A NOTE FROM NOEL

"Anybody who tells you that he has some way of leading you to Spiritual Enlightenment is like somebody who picks your pocket and sells you your own watch."
Alan Watts

Before I give you an insight into my world, there's something you should know: 'I'm not your average Joe.'

I'm not 'one of the masses.' I'm probably considered a little 'out there,' an oddball by those that brush past me, but who never stop to get to know me. I can quite often side with the anarchist, whilst practicing a spiritual life. My purpose is to get you, the reader to begin to change for the better starting with yourself.

- How you think
- How you feel

Ultimately, the effect you will have on others once you remember who you really are and why you're here. When individually we change for the better, it's another click on the hand-counter of collective Love Consciousness.

The more we, as a loving and compassionate human race embrace oneness and shun segregation and division; we raise the vibration of humanity another notch. You can either live in fear, or you can live and act in accordance with love. It's up to you.

DEDICATION

This book is dedicated with heartfelt love to my late friend Anne Marie (Murray).

You were taken from us too soon and I feel sad that I was not there for you when you needed me. You know how much I truly miss you. I'm pretty sure you had something to do with me meeting Tina and for that gift alone I could never thank you enough.

The hurt is over now. I love you and cherish the moment that when my time comes you will be there to embrace me.

Always,

Noel

First published in Great Britain in 2018 by Daisa & Co

The information given in this book should not be treated as a substitute as professional advice. Any use of information in this book is at the reader's discretion and risk. Neither the author nor the publisher can be held responsible for any loss, claim or damage arising out of the use, or misuse, of the suggestions made or for any material on third party websites.

A CIP catalogue record for this book is available from the British Library.

ISBN 978-1-9997894-1-1

Book typeset by:
DAISA & CO
Westfield Lakes, Far Ings Road, Barton upon Humber
North Lincolnshire, DN18 5RG, England
www.daisa-co.com

Printed in England by Clays Ltd, Elcograf S.p.A.

Daisa & Co is committed to a sustainable future for our business, our readers and our planet. This book in your hands is made from paper certified by the forest stewardship council.

CONTENTS

Trust Your Spiritual Sat Nav
E-Book Available

www.spiritualsatnav.com

ACKNOWLEDGEMENTS

I wish to begin this page with a statement that nicely underlines where I currently find myself in direct relation to those whom I have had, and currently have the pleasure of knowing.

'When you dive into Self-Discovery, and seek the Authentic Self, those that knew you for the mask you once wore, can become very disappointed with you discarding it. Whilst it's painful to sever old connections, you must realise that Self-Discovery changes your whole relationship with everything. Not just people, but everything, the whole Universe.'

If you are reading this book and can claim to know me, or have known me, then I thank you. I thank you for being part of and helping me shape who I have become to this day, the good, the bad and the ugly - all of it. Sometimes it wasn't pretty. Sometimes there were tears of laughter and joy; sometimes tears of pain and sorrow. But there was magnificence and beauty in it all.

Please know this; you are all immensely special to me. From my own parents and brothers, right back through my Airforce career days, and ultimately into annals of schooling. You've all helped create and shape who I have become. Thank you. There isn't anybody I would want to leave out.

I wish to thank my publishing team; for their insight, creativity, and enthusiasm. Oh, and their patience too! Without Daisa, Jade and Sarah, this book wouldn't be the gift it has become. Thank you so much. I will always be eternally grateful.

Tina Hogan, my awesome wife. Without your total belief and trust in me, this would never have been possible.

Finally, you – the Reader, thank you for picking this book up and reading it. It is you who changes the world for the better by beginning to change yourselves by stripping away all that you are not. Changing a world for the better starts right here, with you.

Thank you for honouring my writing by taking the time to read it, and allowing my reminders to switch on lights, and open dusty doorways to the 'real you'. Let's get out there and collectively join together with love and peace, it really is the only way!

The strength of a civilisation is not measured by its ability to fight wars, but rather by its ability to prevent them.

EUGENE WESLEY RODDENBERRY

INTRODUCTION

I wrote this book to bring a moment of clarity to the table and lay it out like a pack of cards for you to inspect the elements of what society's thinking of you is and who you really are, and how you can change this and become a cog in the process of transformation.

If you want to control a country, you begin at the level of education. Everyone knows this. You'll struggle to change the minds of adults who will fight the system like I do, but children are the next generation. They can be easily socially radicalised to fight for the protection of what they feel is their existence, which has been artificially fabricated for them through their perceptions.

So it's no surprise then that everything's falling nicely into place at the start of the 21st Century. The 4th Industrial Revolution has begun. It's starting with the young people born after 2000 and once they're in their twenties and thirties, the pace will quicken rapidly until it reaches a tipping point.

I'm concerned about this and where humanity is headed. I'm uneasy about how society is being shaped. I don't see a great future for my eight-year-old daughter in regard to her personal birth right of love and joy and the potential for her to be happy.

Yes, she'll probably know no different, and think everything's just fine and dandy. You and I both know that her life when she's twenty will not resemble ours, our parents, or grandparents at the same age, but I'm not talking about materialistic stuff.

My grandparents saw horse and carts deliver the milk. My daughter may have hers delivered by drone to her roof top. I'm talking more about her state of mind. She was born in 2010, and by the time she's ten, she'll know more about algorithm programming than I do about metaphysics today.

You see here's the thing. Life is now pretty much all rigged, all of it. Over the last few years there's been a technical evolution, that's how life is, but what about how society operates and what about how news corporations operate and how banks work? How medical industries and our own governments function?

Countries today cannot even conduct democratic domestic elections anymore. It's not possible because technology has reached such a ferocious level of social interaction, that it can be easily corrupted by external sources. This achieves the hacker's aim of targeting an individual's ability to perceive and act accordingly with action. But that's just one example, there are hidden agendas at play, and they're meaningless unless the cogs in the machine play ball. The cogs are us!

The ball is rolling, and the world is becoming hostile and dark in select areas with growing potential for more darkness. It all happens because it's engineered to exist by the manipulation of humanity's thinking. We now have to move forward and simply create a world where we don't need a figurehead to lead us behind a disguise of a round table of war hungry politicians. We don't need rich politically trained sales persons to sell us another political cycle of 'status-quo.'

So in order to change and move forward, we all need to 'step up,' acknowledge that this is happening and not run and hide. We are at the chrysalis stage in the caterpillar and the butterfly is not yet promised.

The next years may see the world's skies getting darker, and remember this whole historical political fraud is a worldwide issue. It's all been the *same old-same old* really for hundreds of years. Until not that long ago when society began to silently and deviously alter its agenda and it started to change by attacking our sub-conscious.

The Second World War should have seen the end to such thinking, our forefathers gave their lives for our freedom but sadly no, war still exists; because there's plenty of money left in the business. Yes, you heard me correctly. War – is a cash rich business for some. But that's someone else's book! Today I would dare to suggest that people my age around the 50 mark may well feel like they've been living on a peace time roller-coaster.

If you stop to really think about this new era of the smart phone and the pace in which our human lives are expected to perform then really look at subjects like the threat of war, it's actually a very clever global distraction. If the only thing we're all worried about is war ending our lives, then it's the perfect distraction to allow the global elite super-rich to carry on moulding and shaping their machine...

I would suggest that you don't have to die in a nuclear explosion to lose your life... that's already happening, and it started back in the 1950's. It starts with a trickle flow reduction of liberty and crescendos into a final imprisonment, all wrapped in a pretty bow called 'Orwellian Modern Society.' Basically, you become a prisoner to the system because you're a prisoner to begin with, in your own mind. This is where results from this conditioning really kick in.

This, in a nutshell, is what this book is all about. Can you imagine what it will be like when humanity through sheer blind stupidity relinquishes control to self-programming 'Artificial Super Intelligence' that self-learns and self-programs with absolute power? The global 'AI brain' which will kill off the World Wide Web that runs our future lives... this is when the tipping point for humanity will come, and I feel it's quite literally just around the corner.

If we can all agree that the prospect of a Nuclear War is frightening then yes, that's a given. A Nuclear War is just the end, hopefully painless and quick ... Lights out and goodnight. In circles I mix with the thinking is that maybe starting over again from the stone-age might in fact *not be such a bad idea*. The human race should hang its head in shame at what we've created and the prospects that lie in wait for all of us.

Total global totalitarianism is a long drawn out system of control where you might as well not have bothered turning up. It's society's torture. You're not free. You're not a name any more but treated just like a number. It's taking the principles of military doctrine just that one step further. It controls you and your perceptions about your existence, by creating the grand illusion of freedom and democracy, when the real truth is far from this.

Those battery hens you see on animal cruelty issue documentaries... all lined up in a row with only space to stand and eat. That's where we're kind of headed in a cognitive metaphorical sense. The hen's job was to lay as many eggs as possible for the financial profit of the farmer's business. Our job will be to ensure that the rich stay rich.

This is what I'm concerned about. This is what my daughter is heading straight for. She'll have grown up ripe for the picking; with a 'smart phone' in her little hand, she can be programmed to think – shown constant advertising propaganda – have news channels invent and fabricate 'fake news' so that her perceptions and ultimately her belief system can be 'moulded' to suit the new age of Augmented Life.

Her opinions are formed on the basis of what and how she learns. And as we all know; the zombie youngsters are now well and truly amongst us. Their lives are in that Android Box. We call it a phone, but the word phone, has been lost in translation. They have been placed in another convenient game of divide and conquer, a choice of either Android or IOS, which one is best for you?

Essentially though, it's merely a control box. It started with newspapers which then were superseded by the radio. Then that was taken over by TV. Then saw the dawn of the electronic age and eventually being launched into the stratospheric heights with the internet. Even this will soon become extinct with the take-over from a super hybrid AI global brain.

It's all about keeping the masses fighting over which model and latest gadget to have. Moreover, they are taught that *you've just got to have the latest upgrade.'* Society promotes this. If you're not in with fashion, you're not *'in with the in-crowd'*.

The moment *'Social Media'* was invented, the catalyst for the emergence of total control took one-giant-leap forward. This App has the ability to do exactly what military training does; it's perfect for a vulnerable, impressionable, insecure youngster. It breaks you down, and then builds you back up to surface 'within the system'. *Social-Media* is a ticking time bomb – loaded to the teeth with every negative aspect of life you can imagine. Starting with how it dilutes and manipulates real-time social interaction.

There are kids out there now staring at their phones waiting to see if what they've said is *'liked.'* This will in turn make them feel better about themselves and quash their insecurity about not being accepted. But it's a hit. A quick endorphin fix. It becomes addictive. They spend their whole day transfixed by the power of that next fix, the *'stuff of nightmares'.* As I type this there are young impressionable children out there that become friends with Android Artificial Intelligence. I kid you not. You can now have your very own 24-7 best friend who will listen to your problems and 'advise' you.

I watched a documentary which covered such a scenario where the child went into meltdown, when the residence he was at had no Wi-Fi signal which meant he'd lost connection with his life-line. His AI best friend. Imagine the consequences if that AI best friend could be corrupted? Bearing in mind of course that the child dotes on it and will take everything the Android says at face value, model his or her life choices through their newfound perceptions.

That is much more frightening than any war but it's coming! They can be very easily socially *radicalised* to fight for the protection of what they feel is their existence, which has been artificially fabricated for them through their perceptions.

These will be the ones who see 'AI' as all they've ever known. Global Artificial self-learning consciousness will be to them, like the internet is to us. To them, it will be how we viewed the very first digital calculator. Stone Age, slow and extremely cumbersome.

You see, these new 'Orwellian Age' grown-ups will outnumber us older generation types, and they'll have been under the control of the super-elite head controllers for some time. This is where the tipping point sways in their favour and total humanitarian control on a global scale will see the big switch flick on.

This book addresses and studies *the self* and why you would forever be lost in this modern world if nobody reminded you of who you 'really' are, and what you're capable of. If you want to know exactly why you're probably not 'yourself'... you need to turn your attention on everything out there around us.

THE PLAYGROUND OF SOCIETY – THE BIG FAT LIE

Essentially, for most of us that's what life has become... I'm asking you to save yourselves by opening your eyes and waking up. Do your own research. Read up on what society calls 'conspiracy theory.' Read David Icke's books. Look at some of the topics he discusses. Join the minority now and you stand a chance of fighting the system and stopping this madness.

Don't just do it for you though, or even me. We've had our halcyon days. Do it for our children and their children, they need our help right now!

We install change by changing from within. It begins with you and me. Then, the ripple effect takes care of the rest. The shift in global consciousness begins to gather momentum. Make no bones about it though; there is a great deal of work to be done. Mother Earth needs your commitment to a more loving and peaceful environment, where Love is the new religion and the days of hatred and indifference are consigned to the history books.

The strength of a civilisation is not measured by its ability to fight wars, but rather by its ability to prevent them.

So, I'd like to thank you for listening and for reading my book. It may just change your whole life, which has the potential to change the world. For the better!

Love and blessings,

Noel

*I went off to fight the politicians'
war in 1990 and returned safely
from Saudi Arabia in March
1991... For me, that was a
turning point in my life.*

CHAPTER ONE

Shedding of the Old Skin

"My ego was sat behind a posh glass table and kept arrogantly raising an eyebrow and shaking its head 'tutting.' I so wanted to jump across the table and punch its face in."

My school days were nothing to be proud of. I've got my big boy pants on now, so let's be real here. It was all a bit of a blur and I seem to remember being told constantly:

"Hogan! You'll end up eating out of the bins if you don't stop playing the fool!" To which my thought was always, "But sir, I'm not playing at it? I'm deadly serious!"

So here is my analogy of swimming in the 'pool of life.' Some swim past me with vigour and gusto. Some are frightened to swim past the 2.0 metre marker. Some don't like swimming, and some don't even know the pool exists. Some cannot reach the pool, yet would love to just experience the water on their flesh. They are constrained by mental or physical boundaries, and are just mocked and laughed at cruelly by others with no empathy and compassion. In terms of an analogy I think that's a fair representation of life as we know it. We attempt to put on a confident face but beneath it all most of us are struggling with one thing or another and *'getting through it all,'* as if we were on some game show trying to win a set of steak knives.

My wife knows this all too well. She's an angel, she completes me. A cheesy cliché I agree, but never has that been so true. My wife Tina totally accepts me for who I am and who I want to become. There's no controlling and no judgement, whereby enabling me to be the real me. For instance I'm the sort of person who gets in an elevator in a shopping mall and when two or three other people get in there's this sort of uncomfortable close proximity and stuffy silence. It's at times like this I like to strike:

"Well, thank you all for coming I'm glad you're all here because I've something very important to ask you..."

"Here's what I'm battling with on a daily basis and I really wanted to know your thoughts good people.

When fish are caught by anglers, and thrown back into the river, do they tell all their other fish friends they were abducted by aliens? ... Also, then do all those other fish ignore the fish and call it a conspiracy theory?"

I actually still think it's a valid question, however, moving *'swiftly on.'*

As I write this I'm 49 years of age (and a half). Yes, the big 49 *(and a half)*. I explain the *half* because I'm still a child at heart. It's extremely important when someone 'old' asks you your age when you're four *(and a half)* that you include the half because you are literally counting the days until your next *huge* milestone. When you're young, you want to be older. When you're old, you wish you were young again. The illusion of time has dealt you the Joker card from beginning to end. I think it's the ultimate circle of a paradoxical existence much the same as when you're born.

Everyone is happy and you're the only one crying your head off. When you die however, you're the one with the big smiles as you find yourself floating above your body, and everyone else is crying.

For someone who finds himself writing a book, this chapter is going to be a bit ambiguous. I'm not sure whether it's because I have a very bad memory or, there's a medical explanation. I say medical because like many airmen during the Gulf War of 1990/91 I was subjected to multiple cocktails of 'vaccines' administered by the MOD which we now *believe according to various sources* were never tested.

These have since given many ex-service personnel a cavalcade of horrendous health problems along with their subsequent offspring. However, I consider myself very lucky and extremely fortunate, that realistically speaking, I'm fine. But the memory of my childhood is masked by select pockets of cognitive fog, and doors have been closed to specific events. There are very few memorable events that spring to mind and if I had to describe my schooling days, I'd get a *'See Me! 6/10...could try harder.'*

I basically revelled in playing the fool, and how I actually passed any test or exam is still to this day, something which baffles me. I left secondary school in 1985 to find myself luckily joining the Royal Air Force.

Unemployment during the *Thatcher* years was now at the 3.8 million mark and for most of us looking on at the thought of finding a career it was squeaky-bum-time. But I got lucky. It was going to be a twelve-year joy ride. Nothing was going to really change from school. I would take what I wanted from the experience and just treat it all like a game. I would do this a lot.

But when I was to be older and wiser, I'd realise one day why I never took anything seriously or always played the fool. That however is another page in this book.

The RAF was indeed a fantastic twelve-year journey of experience and to this day I can almost recall most of it. Well, the good bits especially. One particular bit that wasn't at all good was the Gulf War; to my utter shame and embarrassment, I never actually considered *'going to war'* as a realistic chapter in my life.

I joined the RAF on a very naïve career basis. I had no intention of killing anyone, and it never really occurred to me that *'that'* was the end game - I know, how stupid can you be?

I think the clue might have been hidden in all the aircraft and weapons along with the camouflaged uniforms. Everything prior to war was 'practice war' and I never prepared myself for it. So as the first patriot missiles fired that night on Wednesday January 17th *"somewhere at a secret location in Saudi Arabia,"* I went from boy to man in about five sharp seconds, together with a change of underwear. Without this subject easily becoming a book on its own, I went off to fight the politicians' war in 1990 and returned safely from Saudi Arabia in March 1991... For me, that was the first key turning point in my life.

That period in history will ask many questions of the world but it did provide me with a kind of therapy. I actually realised who I was becoming for the very first time in my young 23-year old life. I stopped to think about it. I subconsciously began to join the dots behind me and came up with *The Bigger Picture*. I kind of liked it. But there would be emotional and mental consequences for my part in a dark period of humanity's history-making process. This was something I would have to confront and couldn't bypass.

Fast forward to 1998 and I drove out of RAF Leeming main gates one morning never ever to return. My twelve-year career was done. My last day in the service was cold, unfriendly and had an underpinned anxiety about it that I point-blank refused to acknowledge. I just wish I knew *then*, what I understand about life *now*. Things would have gone a lot smoother.

Hindsight is such a twisted, beautiful yet cruel paradox. Once I took stock of the page of The Book of Life I found myself in, I seemed at first to feel refreshingly happy. I had survived a twelve-year term in the Forces and gave the whole experience 9/10.

Yes, I really missed it and all my friends, but it was now the end. The page had to be turned.

There were elements that if I could have a second go at, yes, I'd change things maybe, but after spilling those thoughts out to a close friend they gave me their take on it.

"You can't change what you've done. You shouldn't regret anything. It is what it is, and everything is significant in the combination of events that are expressly geared toward creating your persona and who you are.

Regrets have no common place here. If you want to examine the experience and learn from it, fine. Change the experience? No Noel. That's not in the script."

One day I found my old *'No. 1'* Dress Uniform with all my shiny medals and ribbon hanging from a bar on the top left pocket. I held it up in front of me as if to size it up in a shop mirror seeing if it would fit. It was at that very moment that I realised who I was! I wasn't someone who wanted to boast about what I'd done, where I'd been and what I stood for. I kind of just saw a label. I didn't see anything else if that makes sense?

I saw one of the masses. I didn't see the *me* I'd hoped to find in that mirror. Don't get me wrong, I enjoyed my RAF career and I did what I was told to do without question. I'm proud of my part in the routine teamwork and framework of day to day flight operations. I lived for it and couldn't get enough.

We worked hard, and we played hard. It was a surreal experience. But now the dust had settled, and I'd moved on. I wasn't someone who felt proud to have been part of a war. The war cannot be re-written. Lives cannot be brought back. That which is done is done. I wasn't someone who revelled in the memories of conflict by proudly wearing his medals on his chest for all to see. To me they were a constant reminder that I had an indirect part to play in the destruction of my fellow human beings - *People*.

No different to my wife or your parents. No different to that beautiful innocent infant in the pram with everything to live for. It wasn't until I found myself away from the noise of a busy career; the aircraft and mayhem, that I had a chance to study myself in solitary thinking and I didn't feel right. I didn't feel good about it. Yes, I accepted it, but to move forward carrying the old feelings which I thought I should have done because that's what I 'thought' society wanted me to do... the battle with myself began. I felt lied and cheated by my own self - I'd woken up.

An emotional bucket of ice had been poured over my soul, and I shuddered at the thought of carrying my past around with me in a backpack like an old car part that had since been replaced. It was heavy, unnecessary, felt worn and dirty. So, I wanted to know who I really was.

I asked myself some pressing questions and studied my current CV. It was the job interview I dreaded. I had applied for the job of being 'who I am'. My ego was sat behind the posh glass table and kept arrogantly raising an eyebrow and shaking its head 'tutting.' I so wanted to jump across the table and punch its face in. My Soul sat next to it and if my soul could have spoken it would have said this; *"Noel Relax! Nothing is under control here. That's just how you're meant to see it!"*

I went and took a lonely walk in a field with my dogs to deliberate. I needed to connect with a 'higher authority', the louder the silence the better. I will always remember that day because when I returned I wasn't the same person. I remember the guilt, the sadness, shame and realisation that I wasn't alone that day when I looked in that mirror. Whilst gazing back at myself in that uniform and those war medals, there was someone else there, maybe a few.

I was overwhelmed with sadness, as if I felt the pain and heartache of thousands of men, women and children who were exterminated by hundreds and thousands of weapons. There had been innocent women and children torn apart by war with weapons which I had a direct part in loading onto those Tornado Aircraft, because it was my job. I felt only shame. Up until that point in my life, I was asleep, walking about announcing to anyone who wanted to know that I took part in that killing spree.

I was proud to be a part of it and hey look! Here are my medals! It rocked me quite severely. I made a frank and sincere decision there and then to change matters. The next day, I took all my medals and knocked on the door of a co-worker at Hornby where I worked in the Scalextric Research & Development Department and just handed them to him.

"Huh? Are these for me Noel? Where are they from? Where did you find them?"

"I didn't find them. They're mine. They are from my former RAF days - Gulf War. They now belong to you. I know you collect them, just don't ask, okay. I don't want to go there. Oh, and I don't want any money.

So now you have four more. I don't need medals to remind me of what I went through and what I saw. I feel uncomfortable about being recognised and decorated for murder. They're yours now."

"Well, yes. But..."

The following week I paid a visit to the Malt House Arcade in Hythe and handed this rather bemused looking lady my uniform. I knew it would be well received by re-enactors who like to re-live military periods. To close this chapter I want to explain that once I had taken those latter steps with shedding the old me, I also began to question many other facets of what I thought made me who I was. Religion being one and by the way... that didn't take too long either.

The next time someone asked me what my belief system was, I simply told them that I have the same religion as God. When left for a response to this, I usually find a moment of clarity and an expression of bemusement. So, it leads them into asking a rhetorical question.

"So what religion is God then?"

I then respond with the answer, "God has no religion." Religion is a word, an invention of mankind; God has no need for a religion. I prefer to follow God's example rather than mankind's dogma. I prefer to receive my rules from God direct, straight from the source rather than employing the services of a mediator. I then know without a shadow of doubt and beyond any question to trust what I feel. What I know, what I understand and believe. Going to a church or labelling me as religious simply states that I don't listen to God; I listen to groups of people telling me what they know and believe about God.

Someone else's interpretation of what is right and what is wrong. I fully respect and appreciate the diversity of cultural religious belief systems up until the point where it begins to threaten the freedom and impose itself on others. You should not infringe another's human right by selecting their path for them. There may seem to be danger in trusting all that comes direct from what you consider to be the 'source', however, once you begin to employ the services of your spirit and let this almighty 'super power' gift you the emotion of wisdom, you will automatically begin to understand what feels right, and that which does not resonate with you. In my opinion, Spirituality is a personal relationship with the Divine Source. Religion is just crowd control.

That's just a sample text of where I am on religion. It's a preview about my own belief system, and I think it's quite relevant and justified, because you need to know what the author thinks from the outset if you are to trust that I have your best interests at heart here in this book.

To sum up, my life was quite ordinary up until a momentary lapse of reason. Around the year 2000 I had an epiphany, a kind of self-enlightenment. Looking back, I somehow knew *(but without knowing how I knew),* that I had myself all wrong. I wasn't who I thought society and traditional thinking wanted me to be. I was kind of pulling in my life contract for review and refreshing it. I was updating and editing it, I didn't know it at the time but looking back it was so apparent. All my life I wore a badge of total insecurity.

From my early days at school it was just all about attention and insecurity.

Soon though, life was about to suddenly aggressively screech around a sharp 'B-road' entry and go across country, something that surprised even me. A road not anticipated, unmapped, unfamiliar. I wasn't going to follow any life model or idea of it, I would discover one instead. I would feel my way. My own inner GPS would tell me what felt right, not what looked or sounded right. And so, it was done, *the shedding of the old skin*. The new thinking had risen like a phoenix and I would never go back. The journey from that moment to today, as I write this book would be the real me, 'warts and all.' And that 'B-road' still has plenty of beautiful sights to see along the way.

Regarding my thinking and the reason why I changed and who changed me? Well... I will state for the record that it was and is my time to simply 'wake up.' I think by the time you finish reading this book you'll be in no doubt as to the exact reasons why life happens the way it does. It happens *'for you'* not *'to you'*. It may well be your time to 'wake up'.

CHAPTER TWO

Your Inner Sat Nav

"And those who were seen dancing, were thought to be mad by those who could not hear the music."

For some, this writing will be nothing more than another brick in their wall of understanding. They're already well on their way to being a complete and true version of their own spirit in human hologram form. But being a Human Being on this earth, and having no idea who you really are, is like being a lighthouse in the desert, awfully bright but really, no use to anybody but yourself.

We all think differently. So, there will always be differing levels of perception upon what it is we're being told by our immediate environment which we have little or no control over. That's where society has nailed us. We are ripe for the picking because whether you're aware or not, you can become a prisoner, but you don't have to be locked in a room with iron bars for a window. You can be fashioned into a prisoner within your own mind, personal space and your thinking, if you allow it.

This all comes about over time as you listen and read what is thrown at you. Observe and digest the bombardment of what's good for you, telling you and advising you how you should think and how you should live your life by other peoples' scripts. But shouldn't that be up to you?

If you keep this program up, you can become a prisoner – from your true self. The greatest gift we were given by the Creator is *Free Will*. Free Will to choose what we want to experience as we live out this gift of life, but mankind is devious and cunning. There are many souls who have come to earth as seeds of the Divine with purest hearts, only to end up corrupted and manipulative. When these souls enter into the business and commercial marketing network, all hell tends to break loose. They soon learn and go about capitalising and cleverly manipulating a basic given life concept that, *'where there's a need – there's greed.'* From the daily news to the gossip and chat magazines, social media and TV advertising, we are bombarded with a war of negative energy.

When you realise and accept that thoughts are energy and you attract what you think, living in a negative environment can become your own personal hell. When you are limited by negativity you only attract negative outcomes, when in truth you have the potential to manifest an abundance of joy and all your wildest desires. You don't have to live in a personal hell, changing that is pretty unscientific and completely straight forward. To help you find that key to unlock your potential, you need to re-evaluate how you give energy to what you perceive. You need to trust that the direction in your life is the right one for you and not be tricked by all the smoke and mirrors.

As a personal insurance policy, all that you see and hear should pass through a Truth Detection filter called your 'spirit'. That's the way forward that will reset your life compass. This book is all about that and more. It talks about the Spirit Science of who you really are and what you're capable of.

You have an inner GPS (Global Positioning System) of your own that tells you where you currently are and a Sat Nav to guide you to where you want to be next. This time though, you don't follow a path created by others. You feel your own separate and individual way because when you learn to trust your Inner Sat Nav, it is never going to trick you.

If finding out why you're here and who you are depends on how you live then you want to be the most authentic version of you, right? You want to peel off the extraneous add-ons and collection of unnatural bits of you that the world has pressed upon you without your conscious knowledge or permission. You want to be the magnet that has lost all the pins, iron filings and paper clips that have weighed you down and prevented you from being able to see the bigger picture, and prevented you, from being the real you.

I can help you with that. I can help remind you of all the things that you've learned to forget. I can guide you back to doorways; to pastures of thinking and concepts of life that you've simply never thought about, or had removed by the constant programming of the world around you. Simply put, lifting the fog within your thought process, in order for you to see the bigger picture about the choices you make, is building who you really want to be. I will show you that above all else, when you become more spiritual by changing your habitual routines and facets of your thinking, you can open up to the concept of feeling your way through life and not following a pre-programmed map.

No matter what our background or upbringing, no matter our intellectual standing in society or financial status, I would dare to suggest that at some point in our lives we take the time to sit and ponder the 'Big Guy', the billion-dollar question, just once. Why am I here?

One day I went for a walk in a beautiful forest and stopped to listen to the trees, something which I love to do quite often. This got me thinking. My life thus far has indeed been quite a variety of interesting job roles and experiences, and if my time were to come tomorrow where I leave this Earth, I would not look back in anger or regret. I would state before the Universe that I gave it my all and that I believe I have pretty much used it up and worn it out for in most part, the greater good. The 'most' part... but I have never got an answer to a burning question:

Why Am I Here? ~ Nobody told me why I'm here.

However, after years of spiritual research the answer to that question may well be built and designed on the fabric of your actions and thoughts that go toward the contribution of you, existing and living a life as an extraordinary gifted human being with potential beyond imagination.

'Why you're here,' is in fact a long drawn out answer under a heading called 'LIFE' in which you play the role of being you. But being you can be a lottery of disguise and illusion, influence and insecurity.

Your life was pre-programed long before you arrived. So, where am I going with this? Remember there are peers and elders on this planet that have mastered the 'game', and quite often maintain an influence over you, stopping you from discovering who you really are through a variety of programming systems and preventing you indirectly from being the real you.

Daily influences through media, news and advertising has programmed you and distracted you by training your mind into thinking in a purely negative capacity. If you actually knew how damaging to your very fabric of existence taking a negative outlook on life is, you'd never watch the news again. Not ever. So, here's the deal... if arriving at the finish line as the ultimate 'you' is the purpose and reason why you're here...

If you had the opportunity to find out who you really are under all the smoke and mirrors, would you want to find out?

- If you were reminded of basic truths about where you came from and where you'll go once you pass over (at hopefully a ripe old age) would you want to know? Would you at last be able to live? Being unafraid of death?

- If someone told you there are organisations on this planet that have every intention of supressing your existence just below the surface called 'potential', and keeping you from the real you, would you want to know that too? Would you want to know how to deal with them?

- If you knew... if you only knew, just how powerful your thoughts were, you'd reduce your very core being to that of stunned silence at the mere recollection of that which you've thought about to date.

- If you knew to what ripple effect your spoken word had on those around you and others throughout the whole planet you'd sit there in sheer horror, never leave the house or speak to anyone again.

- If you knew you could not die, that death is an illusion, and that you are eternal. That you've lived many hundreds, possibly thousands of lives, you'd be amazed beyond comprehension.

We can agree on one thing here and that is that nobody will ever tell you why you're here. However, you are here, and while you're at it, why not live the very best life for *you* that you can?

So, the answer to that pressing question is this - you are here to 'be', but are you:

- *Being what you really want to be?*
- *Is your life more downs than ups?*
- *Would you like more of the ups?*

It's time to change, but only if you want to. When you live your life trusting your feelings about the world presented to you, and not your eyes and ears... that's the game changer. That's going to be the difference for you moving forward. That's going to change your life for the better. Compared to the much younger me, I actually like myself now. In fact, no, wait... I LOVE MYSELF!

Hang on? Did he just say he loves himself?

Yes, you heard me correct, I do. Not in a vain, narcissistic self-obsessed ego infatuated way, but in a way which is all-accepting, all-forgiving and empathic to my highs and lows, my talents and my faults.

'I am - that I am'.

I have a light to shine like you do. I am no different to you. We are the same. You and I are connected, yes, that's right. You could be Black, White, Mixed Race. Muslim, Catholic, Hindu, Atheist, Gay, Heterosexual confused, 'on the fence.' It doesn't matter about labels. You, who are reading this right now, are connected to me. That, as you'll discover is the very beginning to understanding one of the biggest questions for which you're searching to try and find the answer.

We are to each other, what a single wave is to the entire ocean. You, have the ability to write your own 'book of life' as you live it. And the following text will show you the doorway to your own 'B Road.' It is a road you must travel alone and for yourself. Nobody can teach you. You have unlimited potential, unlimited resource, and if you only knew just how fantastic and completely powerful you are as a Human Being you'd be gobsmacked! I cannot teach you anything. All great Spiritual Zen Masters will tell anyone who they confide in that they do not teach. They only show the way. It is for you to walk that path for yourself.

I'm just an ordinary guy but passionate about life, whose quest for knowledge has arrived at this outpouring of text. My bucket is full, and it has to be emptied, I have observed and now collated it, to be able to pass across that which I have pondered. This book is merely all the conversations I have enjoyed with those who I have spoken with over the years.

You kind of know who I am and what I'm about. Now you are about to find out from Spiritual Science and the psychology of life-thinking, who YOU are too. You will see a jigsaw with a hole where a piece should be. That's you. That's what resonates with you. That's your happy place, your 'feeling' that it's right. We are Love, and we are loved. Life is a very precious gift. The day you consciously decide to treat it as such, it begins to become one.

CHAPTER THREE

We are Spirits in a Material World

"Life is no accident. Your life is very much on purpose!"

I'd spent so much time and energy attempting to figure out who I was, making my place in this world and fitting a mould that everyone expected me to resemble, that one day I decided it simply had to stop. If you are the 'real you', you cannot be anything else and so, you have achieved that which you set out to be, the reason why you're here. You cannot search and find that which you already are, only peel back and disregard the layers and facets that you are not.

Understand that *nothing in this book is new to you*. Nothing I am saying is a brand-new concept; you've just got psychic amnesia. As a human you've been programmed to unlearn it. Everything I will tell you, or let's be more accurate here, 'remind you' is not new because you already know it.

You know it and a whole lot more. This is because primarily, from a very early age, you've been learning to forget it, as new 'stuff' has been force fed into your consciousness, modern new age living and daily stresses of a working life, all trampling Spirit Science to its death.

Besides, you haven't really had time to consider this concept. You've been far too busy getting on with surviving, because ultimately, that's sometimes what life appears to be all about.

- We need to stop
- We need silence
- Our survival depends on it

When we stop briefly to ponder, we often get that *'ah ha!'* moment. It just hits us like a smack in the face. That is to suggest we don't actively observe our journey to that point in which we find ourselves. We notice our point on our life journey with an element of shock and stunned surprise quite often further down the road than we would have liked.

It occurred to me one day with the examination of my own conscious mind-set that there exists a human psychology which when observed, actually saddened me. It also frustrated me on others behalf when I observed their behaviour and their *'glass half empty'* approach to life, it made me feel disappointed. Not entirely at them directly as a judgement, but at *'the system'* that has had them fooled. As children we are pre-conditioned and programmed through what we are taught; what we see; what we hear.

Experiencing what life is as a set of rules and how we are expected to live it. This is why different cultures like the Tibetans and Japanese have a very different lifestyle because from an early age, their children engage in traditional life teachings like Yoga, Tai Chi and Meditation. This manifests a much different perspective for the individual and how they view existence.

In some countries and education systems children are sent to school where exams do not start until the fourth grade. The emphasis is on building the child's personality and character and not judging their ability to learn. I think it's a fair statement to suggest that schools *could* teach children much more about life, and how to live a positive path based on Steiner Education as an example, rather than getting them to 'parrot fashion' learn and recite other people's research for the purpose of passing exams.

So much emphasis is placed on qualifying which more or less ensures they get into serious debt along the way enslaving them *by default* through society's rules of the system. It's all happening though, and we accept it. Children are being released into the big wide world with a set programmed thinking, but obviously lack any life experiences thus far. So if you want to change society that's the most accurate way in which to do it. Re-educating adults is a far harder task due to cognitive dissonance.

I find that when you analyse the makeup of mainstream adults it's a combination of their experiences and what they *think*. Or let's be honest, what they've been told to think. After all, you're only what you *'think'* you are, not what other people tell you, you are. But you have more than likely been tricked into a sort of reverse psychology and relied on the perceptions of others to create your own view of who you really are.

Does that make any sense? What you think – you become.

Please get used to reading that!

You also become moulded by the interactions of those whom you choose to hang around with, your best friends, your spouse or partner. Your thoughts aren't always yours.

They're also a combination of someone else's words directed at your ears and thus becoming kind of second hand, sub-contracted thoughts which in turn you will rent out to your mind. You can in some circumstances have allowed other people's characters both physically and mentally to rub off on yours. Sometimes they are tiny facial mannerisms, and other times you can mimic their dialogue or colloquialisms. We really are very adept at soaking up everything around us, especially energy. But we'll get on to that later.

Then there's human perception. Many people hold all manner of various views on life and death, which again can shape and model their day to day living but deep down and more importantly, their thinking.

It makes me feel sad when people are so afraid of death they can't live and become a prisoner within themselves. They are denied the full experience of this gift called 'life' as a human being here on earth.

You're taught to walk around in a social coma, cooperating with society's idea of how life should be. Yes, the news will tell you it's all negative, terror and war, but as you'll read, and I will share with you time and time again, you've got to get past that. You have to see the beauty in all events and understand that even in the darkness there is a perfect balance.

That's what real life is. But measured up for the benefit of a 'higher authority,' not your own.

We only see what our eyes want us to believe.

Eyes are also projectors, however be careful and mindful about what you think. Not all thoughts are yours and hey, if that's the case who's listening?

THIS WHOLE EARTH GIG WAS NO ACCIDENT

- You're born
- You go to schools
- You graduate and get a job
- You must get married or have a partner
- Cats are not a substitute for children
- You work and pay taxes
- Then retire so that you can hang around to die

You actually decided - not God, not your parents but you! Well, not the physical you; the *soul* you. The eternal you, that's wise and extremely experienced in knowing just what you need to nourish your existence. The *'you'* that if you let it, by slowing down your mind and clearing some space, might tell you using a feeling or two, which direction to take. Which decision makes sense for creating a better life for you?

By the way, did you think you chose this book by accident?

Do you think that events in your life are the subsequent fallout from sheer coincidence?

Not so, read on. Your life is very much *'on purpose'* no accident or coincidence. Everything that you have done, will do and are about to do, is forensically planned and prearranged. That concept is truly difficult to get your human mind around, because the very logistics of it all and random possibilities that have the opportunity to become spoilers, are non-exhaustive. As humans we can't even plan a trip to the shop to buy some milk without some unforeseen event getting in the way - so a whole life – just think about it.

This book was planned for me to write whether I liked it or not. It was planned and what's more, it was planned that you would saunter into the airport or book store looking for what you thought would just be *chewing gum for the eyeballs.*

It's time to wake up and examine what the hell is going on here, this thing called life and your part in it, because it is 'very much on purpose' your part and what's more, a very important one. You are pretty special. Yes, you are. You are so much more than a retirement plan. You have a birth-right of love and happiness, abundance and joy. You chose to come here to Earth.

Why would you choose to come here and not be the real authentic fully loaded 5 star you? Of course you would. You've just got a little lost. A little 'distracted' that's all.

Do you want to make this the day it all started to go right?

Do you want life to get better - *your* life?

Have you been searching for an answer, but you aren't entirely sure you know what the question was in which to find it? Well you've stumbled across this book (so you thought*!*) so then, let's waste no more time and make a valid observation.

- You believe when you look, but your eyes can be deceived by trickery. Remember, eyes will also act as projectors, allowing you to only see what you wish to believe.

- You believe what you hear, and your ears are told lies on a daily basis.

- You can believe with taste and smell but mankind is ingenious with modern invention so beware and proceed with caution. It's a battlefield of illusion out there.

You have a super power which *(I suspect)* until now, you have left upstairs in a box covered in dust in the attic. But you *have* used it more than once before, you've simply forgotten all about it.

Remember that time you were driving home, it was late and very dark. You got lost and came to that fork in the road, you felt scared because you knew a wrong choice may lead to travelling in the wrong direction. Fuel was low, your wife or husband, Mum or Dad were expecting you back an hour ago, so you're worried about them worrying, and things aren't getting any better. You drive up to a junction.

The choices are either one of two ways. From somewhere deep within you, you feel an urge to turn left. It isn't so much a voice but a sensation, an emotion, a feeling. If you had to take a guess, this sensation is adding value to your choice and it's not letting up or willing to back down. *Turn left. Turn left. Turn left. Just turn left. Turn bloody left. Do it now - left - not right? Left!*

You go left! You get home safe. It was a 50/50 good guess. It paid off, you made the right choice. You did that. Or so *you* thought it was you.

When our minds aren't rammed full of day-to-day stresses, we actually have space for 'rent'. Believe me when I say it's more valuable than you could ever imagine! Every single human being on this earth has the ability to receive 'guidance' from their *'higher self'*.

This *higher self* is that element of your being that is:

- One aspect in 3D existence
  *(*Physical vibrational human plane)

- One aspect 5D existence
  (Higher vibrational frequency of Spirit Realm)

In short, it's your holistic self, the messenger that has a 24/7 connection to 'home' ~ the Source ~ Heaven God ~ The Universe ~ Paradise, whatever you name it.

Once you begin to re-examine and re-evaluate your life and re-program and trust your Spiritual Sat-Nav, you begin to use that 'cleared out space' you've acquired. Once you begin a journey of positive thought, then your natural gifts begin to kick in and you can start to rely on the 'feeling' of whether it 'feels' right or not, you win every single time.

There's a tick list of bullet points within this book for you to read through as a daily reminder. It isn't some kind of new religion, ritual or cult. It's a list of life reminders that will be absolutely guaranteed to change your gears and get you going in the right direction, not headed down that dark road with low fuel, guessing your way home.

CHAPTER FOUR

The Elephant and the Stake

"If we really want to move on as a human race, and evolve into what we truly are meant to be, we need to change the system."

Once upon a time there was a baby elephant that was purchased to labour on the forest estates in Africa. He was only six months old. His mother had been killed by poachers, so he was all but rescued in effect.

The little elephant was treated and fed well but to ensure he didn't disappear (for his own safety) he was tethered to a large 8' long stake sunk into the ground 2' deep. He wasn't going anywhere albeit within his 30 metre radius, so he could freely exercise and eat from the trees that bore fruit. But that limitation did have its logistical difficulties.

The elephant soon grew up through the years, enjoying his work and became very good at pulling up and carrying 3 or 4, 10 metre long trees down to the river where there was a bridge being constructed. All the labourers adored and loved him. Many years later the elephant being very elderly couldn't work, so the keeper decided the only kind thing to do was to put the elephant to sleep.

There was nowhere to keep him and if they let him go, he wouldn't survive.

That morning a local tribeswoman adorned in a stunning beautiful pink and orange silk dress came from the township with her bag of medicine. As he opened his eyes, the elephant was extremely startled and frightened by the doctor's colours, panicked and bolted, effortlessly ripping the stake out of the ground and ran off into the woods never to be seen again.

At any point during this little elephant's life, he could have taken his stake out from the ground and roamed the forest living a normal joyful natural life. He could have escaped a life of imprisonment, but sadly, he never considered life to be any different from that which he had been taught. He ignored his own instincts and trusted his captors. It would become all he knew.

There's a way of thinking behind this tale that needs little if no explanation.

TEACHING THE RIGHT ANSWERS

Whilst we're all talking about *thinking* let's now look at school. We go to school. What do we think school teaches us?

- Does it teach us about life?
- Does it teach us to think and research for ourselves?
- Does it teach us about love and compassion?
- Does it teach us about the science behind the human body and energy; what we truly are?
- Would it dare to teach us that we are from another place? Another dimension? (Controversial)

I think you'll be lucky if it taught you about banking, taxes, buying cars and houses. No - not at the schools I went to either. The schools I went to were more than likely very similar to the ones you attended.

The basic fundamental idea is that you have to prove that all of the information you are told, you can retain and then one day spill it all back out when questioned during an exam. Are you thinking this is great because you're learning or great because you get to pass the final exam? And what exactly *are* you learning? When you study the concept of what a school is, and then what a prison is, there are very frightening similarities.

Both have the following attributes:

- Authoritarian structure
- Fixed dress code
- Extremely little input or decision making
- A focus on silence and order
- Negative biased reinforcement
- (Older schools) Walk in lines
- Loss of an individual's autonomy
- Abridged freedoms
- Strictly programmed times for eating
- Strictly set times for rest or recreation

That's school. You don't really learn much unless you become passionate about it but at a pubescent age *(in my opinion)* that's not likely to be the case. (Not impossible but unlikely). School is about other 'kids' bringing up your kids and passing exams to be accepted into bigger schools.

The problem here is not children or people being educated. The problem is that they are educated *just enough* to believe what it is they've been taught.

As a profession, when I'm not scribbling away or researching, I'm a Company Director and our unique selling point is Legionella Training. We teach company managers and staff the importance of methods and management guidance in a bid to eliminate or manage risk associated with the threats of bacterial proliferation within water systems. Stay with me here...

During my company-building process I had a meeting with like-minded individuals and the topic was *"Online e-learning"* Basically, you go online and take an exam to gain a Legionella accredited certificate. So, I looked at the online course and whilst it was very good and right for the marketplace I then explained why I still favoured the old tried and trusted methods of personal presenter-led classroom training.

When people learn, why are they learning? They are learning to pass an exam. Okay. So, if they're learning the course content and they pass the exam they will have learnt the answers to the questions, yes?

I don't know about you, but I have an ethos to run my company as practical and credible as possible. When it comes down to Legionella which can kill, I'm not happy about an online exam. Here's why...

In the field of Legionella control there's a psychology at play that nearly nobody ever stops to take on board. Legionella kills. It should never come down to a tick box exercise and answers to questions which, effectively an online course is, no matter how superbly presented and executed. It's never about teaching delegates the answers. It's about teaching delegates to *ask* the right questions.

So, to recap, I teach and train. But I don't teach delegates to pass an exam. They are taught to ask the right questions which in turn will only ever in retrospect produce the right answers. That's what school means in my book. Teaching students to research and look for themselves at the situation that presents itself and, in doing so allowing themselves to automatically know or find the right answers:

- Teaching facts and figures is just someone else's research
- Teaching students to research other's facts and research and how it resonates with them - is teaching

FREE THINKING

Do you remember the previous text where I mentioned thinking and being manipulated to receive information as subconscious thought? Well here are a couple of paragraphs on thinking that's a little more positive. It does though have a twist. A connection to how we perceive our own actions and just how we view society's take on our thought process.

This time, we shall look at our very own thoughts. Isn't it true that during our early years we are taught at school and in social circles that the worst punishment is solitary confinement? To be told to "go to your room," is quite the norm.

Or was it just me?

I recall watching a documentary about a mass murderer housed in the infamous Alcatraz State Prison. I can't remember his name, but I do recall his actions led to his incarceration and were unspeakable to even comprehend. He was waiting for the death penalty by lethal injection - not very nice, you'll agree. A documentary reporter who was about to be escorted into an empty room with just two wooden chairs and a table with armed guards posted in each corner, turned to the camera and explained that this was 'probably the most insane thing he had ever witnessed.'

An interview then took place and the presenter asked the prisoner how he felt about what he'd done, and did he feel any remorse? The main point that I remember was that this man came across as a totally reformed character. He agreed that he deserved what was coming to him and wasn't afraid of death, because he had spoken with God during his isolation and God had told him he was forgiven.

Whether that was just good acting or whether he really meant it I'm not sure. But why lie? What has he to gain from it? He was locked up in an empty cell for twenty-four hours a day and only allowed lone excursion to the exercise yard every four days or so. He only had his thoughts for company, nobody to talk to, not even the guards. So how does someone go from serial killer to devout religious disciple of the Word of God in seven years? He hasn't had a single book to read and hadn't been influenced by any other human being?

We discussed earlier the concept of trickery where you as an individual aren't thinking, the big businesses are doing it for you via your eyes. In the case of this prisoner and his thinking, he had no outside influence at all, literally nothing but his own thoughts.

I would be willing to bet that with very little to contemplate other than his own fate, which wouldn't take up too much time, he was left with an empty mind, a kind of spontaneous daily meditation by default. Just ponder now on the extreme ends of the thinking spectrum using our two examples:

First you have the busy Mum:

- House work
- Shopping
- Maybe additional work outside the home career
- School pickup
- Preparing meals
- Shower and sleep.

Yeah, good luck with time to think on that. That's a real job.

The Prisoner:

- Just empty space

Having all the time in the world to think and often, about nothing; but when you empty that head... there's space for rent remember, it allows information to come in. Not from TV adverts, not newspapers or other people's chatter and influential opinion, but from *'alternative sources.'*

So, here's a random off the grid question for you.

Who's really free, the busy mum, or the Prisoner?

There's more than one answer there from a spiritual perspective.

CHANGING THE SYSTEM

If we really want to move on as a human race, and evolve into what we truly are meant to be, we need to change the system. Not replace it but build a new one that supersedes the old.

It begins with the children. If you teach and program a child as you would that poor elephant shackled to a post, it will only ever know that one circle of knowledge and comfortable surroundings for itself. If we teach children to think for themselves and research, to ask questions, to question belief systems and to accept possibilities as a concept, then together with other topics like meditation we could actually see the end of hatred and conflict. But there is a reason why we are programmed, and we'll look at that next.

If you actually knew... I'm going bold capitals people on this one...

IF YOU ACTUALLY KNEW JUST HOW AWESOME AND POWERFUL YOU ARE, AND LINK UP WITH OTHERS WHO KNOW THE SAME ABOUT THEMSELVES, THE WORLD COULD BE CHANGED FOR THE BETTER.

To have to want to change, you must first recognise a valid reason to need it.

If your *want* is peace within yourself, then you must face the aggression and hostility within your consciousness. Acknowledge it, don't run away dancing with daisy chains in your wake and posting loving affirmations on social media, in the hope that you'll trick people into thinking you have an alternate identity. This is a form of 'spiritual by-pass'.

You cannot take the short cut. You must start at the beginning of what it is that's creating tidal waves within your calm ocean of thinking. If you want peace for all, you must accept and acknowledge that war exists, and we together must strive to generate a flow of love, and a vibration of calm understanding. This should be the catalyst for individual and collective thinking. This is why I wrote this book. This is why you are reading it.

I'm doing the very thing we spoke about earlier. Your thoughts aren't yours, even now as you read this text. Just like the supermarket billboard advert and the busy mum. They're my written text from my thoughts, being read with your eyes and now becoming your thought energy. I'm simply trying to contribute to Mass World Collective Consciousness.

If one-by-one people begin to alter their thinking because they understand that thoughts are energy and the Universe acts on this, then we have the capacity to change our existing world for the better. We are simply holograms of our true selves, *spirits in this material world*. We can change it. We have the power. It's society as a whole that lives in fear. It has its own script, so we are conditioned and programmed from an early age to succumb to a kind of matrix. Our world is unfair, corrupt and there are elements of it that we need to face if we want to change it. But you will always fail to achieve change by fighting fire with fire. You cannot change war with more war. Darkness can only be altered by light, by new thinking, compassion, peace and love.

WHERE THERE IS A NEED – THERE WILL ALWAYS BE GREED

The world today is more corrupt than you could possibly imagine… but the reason you're not aware is because of life aspects and concepts which you've learnt from a young age to trust.

Concepts you've learnt to regard as best friends, when in fact, they are the wolves keeping you locked in your house, or more to the point, *the elephant tied to that stake.*

I'm now going to list in order of my own personal beliefs what it is that is programming and enslaving you because that's what's happening, you are being programmed by:

1. That box in the corner of the front room.
2. Newspapers
3. News Broadcasts on TV
4. Adverts (On TV and billboards)

5.   Radio adverts
6.   All 'social' media
7.   All gossip magazines

The list does go on and there are quite a few very nasty companies out there who you think are designed to help make your life better, when in fact, they're only making you dependent on their products. It's actually all about their profits, not your well-being. You need to recognise your own cognitive psychological shopping list, and the distinct difference between what you're being sold, against what you actually want to enhance your life.

There are also other characteristics of company marketing and mis-selling that nobody really cares to acknowledge or understand.

I'm not trying to sell you this. This whole book isn't designed to alter your belief system or convert you to anything other than your true self. I'm just bringing certain subjects to the front of the stage so that you can see them. I'm giving you a doorway to walk through, so you can have a look around. Please take any of the following and research it for yourself. I can tell you this much, it makes for quite a depressing picture.

This is the only negative downside to knowing stuff you didn't know before, because you're quite literally 'programmed' by the TV and all of the media to 'think' in a very unique and traditional way. A methodology cleverly designed to make you actually believe that being tethered to that stake is good... is safe... is the right thing... *for you*.

We now live in a world where through the sheer greed of the powerful few; we have doctors and pharmaceutical companies that are knowingly or unknowingly destroying our health.

We live in a world where solicitors and lawyers destroy the fabric of justice because it isn't about justice. It's about who has the most financial power to win the case. We live in a world where schools and universities are hiding truths and deconstructing knowledge. Governments destroy our freedom under a disguise of democracy.

The press fabricates stories it wants us to believe in order to distract us from the truth. Banks use our money to destroy our economy and what's more, we let them, then we bail them out and let them do it repeatedly. If you did what they did, you'd never see daylight again. If you're told something long enough, you begin to believe it and before too long, you'll defend that belief with aggression.

That is where it all starts to go wrong for humanity. You are programmed to be numb and not fully awake. Society wants you sound asleep and jumping when they say so and not to ask how or why. But some people don't like to be told the truth. Some even become very angry and even violent in response to an idea that questions what they have held dear.

There's a term called 'Cognitive Dissonance' and here's the definition:

Cognitive dissonance is the mental stress or discomfort experienced by an individual who holds two or more contradictory beliefs, ideas, or values at the same time; performs an action that is contradictory to one or more beliefs, ideas, or values; or is confronted by new information that conflicts with his or her current held belief system.

The world can sometimes appear to be very different when you suddenly and abruptly wake up and smell the coffee. But if you ask most people, everything is just fine. Once you *'wake up'* and see elements of society and our system for living for *'what it really is'*... the ones who remain where they are will label you as the crazy gang, the conspiracy theorists, the nutcases. Me. *I'm one.*

That's what those who want you to walk around like a zombie will call you. Remember, *'those who could be seen dancing were thought to be crazy by those who couldn't hear the music.'*

The more knowledge you acquire about life and what's actually going on, the crazier you will appear to those around you.

CHAPTER FIVE

The Worry Machine

"You do not defend your being. You just know if it resonates with you or it doesn't. Defence doesn't even come into it."

One of the biggest problems about you and me is that we have complete free will to *think*. More often than not this is far too much, especially at night. Just as you begin to feel sleepy; settling down into your welcoming bed you're woken up, worrying about the following day...

You start to go through all of the possible scenarios at the meeting you're going to attend where your boss isn't happy and has called you in... Does this sound familiar?

When I was much younger I used to actually decide what events would unfold given the relationship between scenarios and decisions taken. My mind was like a spin dryer with thirty giant steel balls inside it running at warp speed. I mean holy meatballs! What a racket and for what? What did pre-empting outcomes achieve, except worry and a headache?

This is totally and utterly pointless, like smashing up a lifeboat to build a raft. There are no such things as problems really. They aren't real things. They're merely a product of your anxiety based on your perception of a scenario not unfolding as you anticipated.

Something goes wrong, or, it doesn't appear to go *'the way'* you thought it would. So, you begin to think and worry about it. Worrying about it begins to fill your mind and prevent any possibility of coming up with a tangible solution and so... it just keeps going like a line of tumbling dominoes.

Then, some smarty pants says to you:

"Hey, just stop worrying about it! Relax!"

Fun Fact: Nobody, and I mean nobody, has ever stopped worrying about something when told by someone to stop worrying!

So, let's get right to it if we're talking about thinking or thoughts. Why the fuss? What's the problem here? Why are we even entertaining this topic?

If you didn't know already, there's a scientific standard given that you are 'energy'.

The entire Universe is made of energy, and your body is no exception. Long before modern technology and science, ancient cultures knew that all living things carried a life force within them. Chakra is an old Sanskrit word that literally translates to 'wheel'.

According to the dictionary, the word Chakra means any of the points of spiritual power located along the body. In a healthy, balanced person, the seven main Chakras provide exactly the right amount of energy to every part of your body, mind and spirit.

The study of Chakras is a subject you might enjoy researching.

So, if what you are is made of energy, then what about what you produce? What about your thoughts?

Who's listening?

- Anxiety is fear
- Worry is anxiety
- Thoughts are energy
- What you think - you create
- Fear is in opposition to Love
- What you think - you become
- To fear attracts fearful and negative energy
- To fear sends out the wrong signal to the Universe

Living as a beautiful human being on this earth you have two possible choices. You either act out your life choices in thoughts or actions in accordance with:

- LOVE
- FEAR

It's *that* simple. I've no doubt you may be somewhat perplexed by that, so I'll ask a question on your behalf to whoever is listening.

If thoughts are energy, I'll ask again - who's listening? And what's this 'sending out signals idea'? Who's the signal to - and who's going to receive it?

Universe: *WE ARE!*

You: Who are *we* please?

Universe: *THE UNIVERSE*

You: You mean The Universe is listening to what I think?

Universe: *Indeed, all of it, your thoughts and your words. What you read, think, speak, everything that in turn passes through your thought process.*

You: So, I'm being spied on? Is that it?

Universe: *Maybe, if you want to think of it in a negative context that's up to you.*

You: What are the alternatives?

Universe: *You need to find the answer to the question: What is the opposite of negative?*

You: It's positive?

Universe: *Correct.*

You: So, if you're not here to spy on me - then what?

Universe: *You decide. You have free will. You are free to choose. But you must choose wisely. You have already read, 'what you think – you attract.' So why would you think negatively? Why not think positively?*

Then you will attract only positive experiences within the life that you chose to live.

It's a combination of attracting what you think through thought and also, reaping what you sow through deed.

You: Ah, right. I think I get it. Thank you, Universe.

Yes, the problem is we think. But we also have the capacity to listen and turn what we hear into thought. Recycling and digesting everything that's thrown at us by all of the electronic media we have around us today, because that isn't you thinking that you're thinking. That's you receiving input disguising itself as *your* thoughts when in fact, it isn't, it's someone else's thought injected into your consciousness and more importantly, *your* subconscious.

Remember thoughts are energy. Whether they are yours you've created, or others that have been fashioned into word or text, and when you read or hear them, they're sent out into the Universal void as yours. This will have a direct bearing on what you attract into your life, so choose what you think wisely.

We address this here under 'manipulative thinking'. Manipulative thinking is in its simplest form *thinking for you on your behalf*, because *'you are what you think.'*

You can be manipulated to become someone totally different to the person you really want to be. You are simply 'following' a path and not stopping to be allowed to *feel* if it is right for you and to think for yourself.

An example of this is listening to the news on Radio or TV. You aren't thinking, you're listening to other's energy and you're laundering it. When you hear a voice or read words, does it feel right and resonate with who you are? If you don't know because you feel confused, that's telling you something different altogether. It's telling you there's a blockage between your heart and your head chakra.

Don't panic though!

This is extremely common and can be fixed. If your bucket (mind) is full - no more capacity to refill, you need to empty out the old such as all those negative news programmes, gossip magazines and that social media page which is nothing but idle chatter. You'll always find space if you need it. It's just that you never actually stopped to realise you needed it.

A SOCIAL AND COMMERCIAL BATTLEFIELD

Advertisements and social propaganda is quite literally a social and commercial battlefield out there; from the daily news corporations, to the shelves in the supermarkets trying to sell you poisons to feed your children.

You buy this stuff because the adverts tell you that above all else, 'they care!' You should always remind yourself about the word: 'care'. Do large companies care? Do they actually as a group care about your health or your child's health? Or, do they stand on the *bank roll* ticker-tape graph of productivity kind of care. The profits and margins shareholder and bonus kind of care?

Companies will design billboard and market products with compassionate TV adverts to get your attention. To make you think... but care? No, not really. In the majority of cases I'm inclined to suggest it's all about the money. Don't get me wrong, I'm not knocking good business. I'm just saying to you; keep in mind what the bigger picture looks like.

Remember the end game is PROFIT. Compare what you're being sold to what you originally want to purchase. The classic examples of clever hypnotic marketing strategy for me are the hair and beauty products. I would love to know what the next big chemical is going to be called where they state with complete proud authority is 'new and improved.'

Silky smooth hair, now with 'peptotron-euroformide!'

That doesn't actually exist by the way. But then again, I'm pretty sure it doesn't matter because the formulas stated on the glossy ads don't either. I've used the search engine for all of these super fantastic new 'eureka' formulas that claim to fix this and that, they simply don't exist and are marketing ploys to add extra 'zing' to products to sway your thinking.

I think the other area is the home upholstery market, the never ending back to back sales. You know the sale that makes no room for normal routine prices - which is clever. The truth is there's no sale at all. It's all a marketing strategy to get the less evolved mind into thinking you're *saving* a thousand pounds when in fact; you're just *spending* a thousand pounds. Simple!

I once shared with a few people what went on in boardroom meetings, about selling strategies and target audience and they thought I was nuts. In fact, it's all quite intelligent clever marketing and I applaud it as a Company Director myself. The point though is who knew? Who actually knows what's going on behind the scenes? Because once you wake up to stuff like this, you can begin to guard yourself from the onslaught. But when you've learnt to feel what's right, there's no defence required.

Supermarkets implement different strategic targeting areas and one of them is children, with tantalizing chocolate and confectionary on 'lower reachable' shelves. You have undergone a psychological evaluation by these companies before you go shopping, I bet you didn't know that but hey, nobody is breaking any laws here.

Here's another subject you can research, a very nasty Neurotoxin which is given to us all through our water. *(This is yet another attack on you by the 'system' to keep you asleep).*

FLOURIDE:

You'll have been schooled to think it *protects* your teeth and so want to actively put it into your mouth, which always make its way into your system. And just guess which part of your body it makes a beeline for? The Pineal Gland. Here's my findings, however please do research it yourself.

"If you still believe the myth that fluoride is good for your teeth, think again. There are a vast number of scientific research studies confirming the opposite – that fluoride is a toxin that is extremely detrimental to your body, your brain, and even to your teeth. One of the most active research areas today is fluoride's ability to damage your brain.

Recent human studies from China have confirmed the results of previous animal studies; that elevated fluoride exposure leads to reduced I.Q. in children. Cognitive ability is further reduced if your child is deficient in iodine. Prior to this, more than 30 animal studies produced since 1992 have reported impairment in learning and memory processes among animals treated with fluoride. Even at levels as low as 1ppm (part per million)."

Studies have demonstrated direct toxic effects on brain tissue, including:

- reduction in lipid content

- impaired anti-oxidant defence systems

- damage to your hippocampus

- damage to your Purkinje cells

- increased uptake of aluminium

- formation of beta-amyloid plaques (the classic brain abnormality in Alzheimer's disease)

- Accumulation of fluoride in your pineal gland

  (Sources: Fluoride Action Network)

Well... well... well! If you even mention 'fluoride' in spiritual circles it tests the metal. Gets us frustrated and angry at the system. Many of us are constantly fighting the system on a daily basis to ensure that we can at least use one of our most natural bodily functions.

Are you starting to see a pattern? Are you beginning to see the bigger picture yet?

- You've been numbed down by chemicals and programming. In a nutshell I ask you to research ~ research and research.

- Question the system. Question what you have been taught. Uncover the cover-up. Be empowered and informed. Be AWAKE. It will serve you well.

Newspapers and news reports are very quick to jump on the 'negative train' and only tell you the negative stuff. But when someone dies, even if they've committed the ultimate sin, there will be those there to talk about their 'good qualities'. You were never shown that though.

When you die, and you give your body back to the Earth, nobody is going to say at your service, *"Oh, he had such an expensive sports car. Oh, and that yacht. The millions in the bank... that's what made him such a kind and lovely soul."* To some false people, that's exactly what will attract friends. But in life, we only ever take with us what we have given away. Isn't it a real shame that we have to die for others to talk kindly of us? Isn't it a shame that we say, 'rest in peace' when we could start now and 'live in peace'.

This book is centred on spirituality. It has absolutely nothing to do with religion or any of your current beliefs. Spirituality isn't about drinking green tea and sitting in the lotus position for hours and hours chanting mantras. That's just an advanced element of enlightenment practice chosen by masters. It's all about living your true-life purpose in accordance with the Universal life force that we are all part of, which I see as *Love, Kindness, Compassion, Trust and Empathy.* The positive ingredients that build the best relationships are these, for humanity to foster love and caring. As Metallica and The Beatles state quite clearly, *'All you need is love, and nothing else matters.'*

As my good friend Aeva once said to me.

"You do not defend your being. You just know if it resonates with you or it doesn't. Defence doesn't even come into it."

As well as being manipulated by a tsunami of thoughts about what you see and hear, you can also be distracted too. The next time something big is all over the news, have a little research session. Have a look at what else *'would'* have made the news. The evening prior to 9/11, a statement was made to the effect that something like Six Trillion Dollars couldn't be accounted for at either the Pentagon or the Federal Reserve. You'll be surprised to know that it didn't make the headlines the next day.

Life can soon become a conveyor belt of acceptance of the status quo before too long. You don't need to think anymore because you've slipped into the deep sleep of mainstream social acceptance. Everything you're being told, you trust.

Why would you question it? It's what everyone else is doing - right? It's what they taught you at school. It's what Mum and Dad were taught, and they emphasised this, by teaching you. That's how life is and shall be for ever more – ah-men! Well, actually, no. Once you become a prisoner of society's idea of who they want you to be and not *who you want you to be*, it's a slippery slope, and one which you'll never question or self-examine.

You'll just head down and plough on given that the cards you've been dealt are the way it is. But if you stop, breathe and listen, stuff starts to happen. Then if you begin to join dots and question beliefs and teachings about what the news tells you and what other people say without asking yourself if it feels right, you're in the minority. You must be a little loopy, right? A nutcase - a conspiracy theorist, yeah, that's always a good one.

CONSPIRACY THEORIST DEFINITION:

A contemptuous term used primarily by the main stream media to slander anyone who questions their monopoly on truth. Even though he has done his own research and has concluded that the official account of events is either lacking or inaccurate, he is still a conspiracy theorist because he does not believe what the main stream media proclaims to be the truth.

Many commercial companies spend countless sums of cash on training their staff to embrace change and be flexible to the fiscal climate of customer needs. Adapt to the market. Growth through change is vital for company profit margins and shareholder annual bonuses. Yet, individually we do very little to review our own standing in society, in our own business, OUR LIVES.

Life changes from day to day, why aren't we having our own meetings with ourselves and asking questions like:

- What do I still believe in?
- Has there been a continual negative attribute about my character that I present but I never realised it?
- Who do I support in the political arena?

- Have I ever stopped to revaluate this? After all, it's not the same people because the party have changed personnel over the last thirty years.
- Does what they state as a 'policy' resonate with me?
- Why do we shop where we do?
- Why do I do the job I do?
- Why are those people my friends?
- Why do I go to church?
- How do I feel about religion and my inherited beliefs from my parents?
- Why don't I paint? It makes me happy, but my partner won't let me?
- Hang on? Why am I married to a partner who doesn't want me to have what makes me happy?

The list goes on. Basically, we've never stopped to re-evaluate in order to create a better life for ourselves. If I had to choose my top number one rant, it would be this:

Society has become addicted to telling young people that they are not beautiful /handsome or skinny enough via gossip magazines and glossy TV ads and so called 'TV Reality' shows.

I have a friend who was told at a very young age that she suffers from 'Body Dysmorphic Disorder' and so; to this day she has convinced herself that she is ill. She has more or less instructed her body to become ill, all because one doctor decided to label her. She is in fact a gorgeous, beautiful woman who simply had anxiety issues and felt insecure. More than likely heightened by watching programs on TV that sold her the idea she wasn't good enough. You look in the mirror and you don't like yourself. You don't like the way you look.

It begins with a lack of self-esteem which leads to lack of self-like and self-love. Congratulations you just completely ruined a life that had the potential to be anything but ruined. It will now take a multitude of people and organisations, time and money, to try and put that right and let's be honest here, that isn't likely to happen. If that person knew and could digest the magnitude of those flippant hurtful words and the repercussions it would have on the rest of humanity they'd take it all back and be on their knees begging to be forgiven. That grinds my gears and makes me very angry. More important is the fact of knowing why it makes me angry which is what this book is about, finding out exactly who you are and taking that forward to create a better life for yourself.

The one key important question that always comes last to:

- Sight
- Sound
- Smell
- Taste

How does it make you feel?

Learning to put that at the front of your dash board as you drive through life will serve you well. When confronted by unknown territory, ask yourself and listen with emotion to your inner Spiritual Sat Nav. How do you FEEL about this?

What you think you attract.

Thoughts are energy.

Positivity attracts positive events.

CHAPTER SIX

The Catalyst

"At any point in your life, you can start afresh. You are not defined by who you have been. What defines you is who you are today - right now."

Before we start on this chapter, I want to draw on my favourite 'analogy for life.' Life is a blank canvas. So, from the minute you are born, you can paint anything you want. The biggest problem in our lives is nobody reminded us about one important aspect of painting our lives. If you 'think' you've finished your master piece, the paint has long since dried and the picture mounted and framed but there's something you've forgotten about - probably the most important part. If you're not happy with it, then why not just start again and paint over it?

I have a motto in life which I like:

"It'll always work out right in the end...

If it isn't right... then it isn't the end."

Picasso painted 'The Blue Room' and when they subjected it to infrared prior to cleaning; they were gobsmacked to see another portrait of a mystery man underneath. At any point in your life, if you're not happy with how your painting is looking, then start another and paint over it.

There are a multitude of subject headings to consider when you want to review your life and look at who you are and where you're going. Your Spiritual Sat Nav just needs an address and you're off. Remember though, don't just follow it; *feel* it. Always ask yourself if the journey 'feels' right not just if it 'looks' or 'sounds' right.

Let's begin then with perception. Not just yours but how and why you think other peoples' perception of you is critical to your wellbeing and your statement of who you really are. Please listen to what I am about to tell you:

Other peoples' opinion of you is actually none of your business. (Yes, I just said that).

Sorry, harsh as it may sound, it's a fact. It's something that you'll have to adopt as a given if you want to improve your life. You must learn this concept and once you ride with it on a daily basis you'll feel quite liberated.

People are either going to like or dislike you but the best part of that is that it has nothing to do with you. There are those who like you for who you are. There are those who like you for their benefit as long as their liking of you serves their agenda. There are those who dislike you because they either want to be you, or your persona reminds them of their own short comings.

But there we go again, *'their short comings.'*

It's all judgement of the self or judgement of others. Instant judgement is a very natural emotional discharge which you learn as a young child and drag it kicking and screaming with you into adulthood. It's a toughie to abandon I can tell you. It's the dirty cousin of the 'ego.' Judgement is a natural human emotion, however here's the key to overcoming this:

It's not the actual judgement but the resulting treatment of them that matters.

- Are you qualified to judge another and then treat them according to how you think they compare to you?
- Have you walked in their shoes? Are you aware of their motives for their actions and could you be empathic about them? I suspect not.

Judgement is a kind of relation to a bigger stronger playground bully who governs all and takes no prisoners. Judgement has a close friend, the 'ego'.

THE HUMAN EGO

The Human Ego is actually quite a tough concept because it doesn't actually exist. It isn't operational until you give a scenario or event your energy in a judgemental fashion. It's on permanent standby. For an example, looking at a lady driving a Ferrari and muttering something like:

"Look at her all dressed up and flashy. Bet she's only driving that because she's married a rich man."

Your ego suddenly manifests itself and then a whole cavalcade of emotions can be plucked and thrown at that woman with absolutely no reasoning other than to define who YOU are.

Hang on? I thought this was about tapping into your standby ego and then judging that person? It's about her, right?

No.

It's actually all about *you*. No – really? Yes, it is!

How you respond to any person, is a reflection of who you are, negative or positive, not what they are. The sooner you put this into your Spiritual Sat Nav the better. It will serve you well and as time goes by you will soon discover amongst other things that it reshapes your thinking.

So, what have we learnt here already?

- *Other peoples' opinions of us are none of our business*
- *Treating others in any other way than how you'd like to be treated via a judgement is a reflection of YOUR personality, not THEIRS*

I just want to touch on other peoples' perceptions of us before we move forward. There's a fine balance between not giving a 'hoot' about what people think of you and getting through life's journey without being cast out to sea in a bathtub. When we say 'don't pay any attention to others' opinions' it is simply that. Keep doing what you believe is the right thing to do, live your life according to your agenda and your truth. Simply stop giving energy to worry about what other people think.

To worry about what others' think is a negative emotion. Negative biased emotions are also negative thoughts. Negative thoughts attract negative events. All you do is waste energy.

PLAYING THE VICTIM

Playing the victim is like firefighting with petrol. Believe me if you want your life to start improving there really is only one door to walk through and it's marked 'Positive Power'. You must know someone who fits the profile? I know I do and I used to know him very well because I was that person, always moaning. Always *'what's the point'* and wondering why life kept knocking me down time and time again?

Life's generous like that. It's extremely good and efficient at delivering what you ask for.

You: "Life sucks. What's the point?"

Universe: *"Yes, it does. Oh, and seeing how that's a thought, a statement of 'who you want to be' and what you are about, here have some more to suck on!"*

You: "Life's a gift. Oh wow. Look at that amazing sunset. Life sure is a gift. What a privilege to witness such beauty. Oh, damn, I've lost that £10 note I need for the fish & chip supper. Oh well, I suppose I can afford it. Many folks have nothing. Not to worry."

Universe: *"Gee, thanks very much. I'm flattered. I think I like this. Have something else nice to be grateful for! You say thanks and I'll keep you topped up with gifts to be thankful for. Great game, Love it! Oh, by the way, last Wednesday you bought a £2 Lotto ticket - yes? Here, have a £25 lotto win - you're most welcome.*

In essence it's the law of attraction being personal. It isn't about stuff, material things or money. *Feeling* who you are is *being* who you are. You don't 'be'. You feel. You are the sum of all you think and feel you are.

What you think creates who you are and in evolving terms, who you are 'becoming' because it's an eternal process. So, to feel totally miserable tells the Universe that firstly you don't like or want to be happy. Secondly, depending if you've mastered the Law of Vibrational Attraction, you'll get much more of it to be even unhappier about. Right, let's get to the nitty gritty shall we. How is this all relevant? How will this change who I am and make my life and direction better?

Okay, I'll begin. At school, the only thing they teach you that comes close to my core book subject is that we are all something like 95% water – fantastic! So, given that you're here and reading this, you're searching for answers. We are not just five-foot eight cucumbers with anxiety issues.

- We are Consciousness
- We are Spirit
- We are Soul

These *were* a singular, but when you were born they split into three so that you could be a lower vibrational 'being' of energy. When you die, (but you don't die, you cross over), you go back to being the 'one self.' As a human being, you are energy and you, like all things, vibrate at a set frequency. Like a helicopter rotor blade on full power. So fast in fact, you cannot see it with the human eye.

It's a pretty heavy subject to get into and without sounding like I'm diluting my responsibility as an author, I would suggest you search *'Spiritual Vibrational Frequency'* and see what pops up. I think if you understand basic physics you will know about Electrons and Neutrons, Atoms and Quarks etc.

That being said; all things vibrate like an electron whizzing around and depending on the 'nomenclature' of different materials, will depend on the vibrational characteristics of that object, living thing or person. So, sticking with the vibrational thing, there is a law of attraction. Spirit Science states that if you match the vibration of what it is you need, (what you desire) the Universal Law of Attraction will kick in and 'manifest' itself one way or another. It's not so much if - but when.

"What you think – You attract".

Thoughts are energy. Positivity attracts positive events.

Just start with that. Things will improve massively I can promise you. When you were conceived, your soul travelled into your body not immediately, but after maybe some weeks from the 5th dimension prior to your arrival. There's not really any hard-core evidence to support an exact theory however, many NDE experiencers who have died and come back have brought back with them 'round figure' estimates as to the timing and methods in which we arrive to take up our physical journeys.

Okay. So now we're born. Birth can be a very short and tragic experience for some tiny babies and a devastating period in life for a mother and father. To accept the loss of what they had begun to love whilst their little one was tucked up inside the mother's womb is heart-breaking.

Sadly, and tragically birth can be short lived, and many mothers and fathers find themselves mourning their loss. It isn't something I would want to discuss because it's far too upsetting and a subject that requires the very best professional and compassionate sensitivity.

There is a Spirit Science at work though, and in a few paragraphs, we'll address why such a sad event would happen and the possible reason for it.

We are originally from a place that people who go to church would call 'Heaven'. I have no problem with this word at all. I also have no problem with other religious terms like Jesus and God. I made my mind up prior to this writing that I would steer clear of religion as a chapter or debate it. It's not for me to discuss. The only piece of advice I would give based on my knowledge of religion is this:

Be exceptionally mindful of a belief in any religion which promotes division between the beautiful diversity of mankind.

God though is a curious and awe inspiring fascinating subject. I personally see God every day in others. In the love they share, the light they shine and the good they do to their fellow brothers and sisters. To me God is in the flowers and trees, the beauty of nature and the animals. God is in everything. We are seeds of God.

God isn't a bearded man with a 'Gandalf' type rod of justice casting 'sinners' into a pit of hell fire from his cloud above, as many pastors and priests might have you believe. But that's just me, just my take on God. I call God the Source, sometimes, the Divine.

Before we arrive on Earth, we live in our true home in the Spirit realms. There are many of them according to who you truly are in spirit. You still have a body but it's 'a body of light'. You still have a sense of who you are, and your personality is the same. You still feel like an individual. You still have your sense of 'being'. If it has evolved here on Earth then what you have evolved into will go 'home' as your consciousness. You will only be richer by that which you have given to others. Not which you have taken for yourself.

What you will not take with you:
- Health issues
- Amputation problems
- Heartache & Sadness
- Hatred
- Jealousy
- Judgement
- Greed
- Resentment
- Addictions
- Pain (The list does go on)

What you will take with you:
- Love
- Compassion
- A sense of humour
- Acceptance
- Freedom
- Amazing sensual upgrades with 360 vision
- Knowing
- Abilities to travel at the speed of light across Universes
- Full knowledge reboot (Amongst other things)

As a reincarnated soul you make choices. This is where we go back to our tragic birth/death scenario. Once you return home in the light of the Holy Spirit/Divine/Source you are a team player.

Ultimately, you are part of the team of the Universe. You are connected to all living things. But to keep things in a perspective which you will understand, you have a splinter group:

A soul family – there could be ten of you or thousands.

Within that group you have 'guides' and other wise elders who you can call on at any time to advise and take council with. Many of these are in fact the Spirits who you didn't believe in whilst you were in a human body, but nothing's actually changed. They are still there guiding you and orchestrate with you and your fellow team of souls how your life is going to pan out.

For example:
- When you will meet your wife/partner
- What is your life purpose?
- To experience what, and to learn what?
- How you want to die

- Your job(s)
- The painful scenarios and the joyful ones

You will engage with other souls to assist you to experience things like mountain climbing, singing lessons, *bank robbery*, divorce etc. the good, the bad and sometimes the downright ugly. There is absolutely no end to the list of possibilities of what you can experience as a human being. You undergo these events as a human to create the conditions of pain and suffering for another human.

You may even agree to be a baby, born for only minutes, and in the eyes of society and family, to tragically die. Because it is a form of pain and suffering that you cannot experience in Spirit. But you agreed to do this. You may wish to play out this awfully painful scenario for someone that you truly love with your core being. But whilst you have *'psychic amnesia'* and can't possibly entertain that kind of agreement whilst you're here in body, it's a concept very difficult to entertain or grasp. Many have great difficulty with it. But that's okay.

Now let's begin to widen the doors to this room of knowledge and explain further. I want to go to a subject that is absolutely guaranteed to throw a thought grenade into the room, pulling the pin and shutting the door with a slam!

CHAPTER SEVEN

Time and The Law of Attraction

**"You can only think in this one moment,
which is all there ever is."**

Is time real? Is tomorrow real? Can you prove it to me? Show me... Can you prove to me that yesterday happened? These are the kind of conversations that you should avoid when you and your friends are down the pub and you're on your third pint. It isn't going to end well without some sort of mediator stepping in. I will make it easier for you, shall I? Time is simply a human concept - a word. There's no acronym that I'm aware of however, what if I made one up for you right now?

To Imagine Myself Eternal

How about that? It actually would work when you consider that TIME doesn't really exist in the world of Spirit. Time is an illusion, as we have become to understand it by the rising and setting of the sun. Time is the justification for the human brain to conceptualise the rationale between birth and death with 'life' being anywhere in between. This is achieved by creating gradients, utilising measurements of movement between the Sun, Moon, Earth and formation of the stars from our view point.

Early civilisations broke those measurements down into years, months, weeks and days, hours, minutes, seconds and hey presto now we have TIME!

"Hey Noel, how about a trip to Twickenham next month for the Six Nations?"

"Hell yeah! See you on the 23rd and meet you at the Red Lion for the coach pick-up."

So, in my mind I have projected a thought forward to a number and a day that corresponds with a pre-planned event. I have manifested time within myself, my consciousness, for myself alone.

I think the easiest way to put this 'time' thing to bed is this. Firstly, I want you to look at your watch.

Oh. It's stopped. The battery is dead.

Question:

- Has time stopped? Or, has a mechanical device representing a concept of time stopped?
- Has it stopped only for you?
- Did anyone else's time become interrupted or did it delay them?

If you took away everything on this planet that depicted gradients of time like watches, clocks, calendars, phones, laptops... basically, anything which 'tells us the time', you'd be left with the basics. This being the sun appearing to rise and set due to the axis and rotation of the Earth, the stars position in the night sky and the colours and condition of nature due to the seasons. But if you move to places near the North Pole, you'd narrow it down even further.

At latitudes of 66.6 degrees or more there are days where sunlight is experienced for 24 hours. Scientifically speaking, when Antarctica is tilted toward the sun around September 21st to March 20th, summer in the Southern Hemisphere sees the sun overhead continuously. It circles the horizon starting around March 21st and does not rise above the horizon until the following September which roughly equates to six months.

It's simply not the same everywhere you go. If you had no modern devices you would live as the ancient Inuits did, a long way back in history.

In Spirit, 'TIME' is a human invention, a human concept... it simply doesn't exist. Spirit world time is a single eternal moment, an impossible reality here on Earth because we like to plan and organise.

There have been a multitude of NDE experiencers who have had great emotional trouble dealing with the fact that they know the hospital records show they were *clinically dead* for forty-five minutes. However, what actually troubles them isn't so much the idea of being dead, far from it. What really gives them a lifelong migraine is trying to equate their experience of 'time' in Spirit to the time they were dead on Earth.

So then, let us examine this difference. If time only exists on the material third dimensional plane but not in Spirit, we haven't really left our home. Well, actually that is true because it's a Spirit Science fact that although we have bodies, a part of our spirit has one foot *(so to speak)* in this realm and the other in the spirit realm. It acts as our speed dial to our landline spiritual home.

When you 'rubber stamped' your Soul Contract with your soul family and slid down into Earth's fun fair, you left your true home in your rear-view mirror. But before you left, you and your tribe knew 'something' you would erase from your knowing and this was that you wouldn't be gone long, and you would forget everything.

LIFE IS OVER IN THE BLINK OF AN EYE

Did you ever spend a few hours sitting in a waiting room? Or have to hang around for some event to pass and not actually be a part of it whether joyous or sad? Took a while didn't it. Clock watching... boy oh boy that day sure did drag, like sitting on a plane for seven hours without a decent book to read. Time is the grandest most magnificent illusion of our entire existence.

There are select accounts from NDE experiencers that tell of a choice on the way back into the spirit realm. They explained that they were asked if they wanted to proceed or take up another life and existence as a human for another immediate experience.

That's how it works. There are trillions of souls all on a merry go round of spirit home, Earth and back again.

So, what do we know now?

- The Spirit World (other realms of existence are available) is our true home and Earth is a brief experience of life.

- We choose our life

- Our parents - our experiences

- What we think – we attract

- Life happens for us - not to us

- We are vibrational beings made of energy

- Time on Earth is an existence within a single moment - nothing more

- Time is a human concept and doesn't really exist

- Life seems long when you're young - very short once you're old

- It's actually only a single moment

- You move along time - time doesn't move along for you

- Oh and you are awesome - a seed of the Divine - that's the important bit

THE LAW OF ATTRACTION

'I AM'

The most important statement you will ever make to the whole world; the whole Universe is 'I am.' What precedes that is up to you. But be very mindful of just what.

The key to the emotional and relationship side of being a human, begins from within. This is something which sadly, nobody ever teaches at school. It starts with you. If you cannot accept who you are and love yourself, then you will find out pretty quickly above all else that sexual and emotional relations between you and your chosen opposite are going to hit the rocks at some point or another. This also extends to friends and family.

Here's what you need to know first and foremost:

- YOU are amazing
- YOU are awesome
- YOU are a seed from the Divine Spark of Creation
- YOU and your place on this Earth is of significant importance to the whole Universe

Did you get that last bit, 'The whole Universe' thing? YOU add value to more peoples' lives than you could possibly imagine. YOU are more powerful than you can ever comprehend. Now then, let's play a game. I want you to go and find a mirror and do something which is regarded as one of the most difficult things we can try and do.

Look at yourself in the mirror and repeat after me. "I Love You".

Tell yourself and mean it. As you will feel and see, it sure is a toughie. Loving ourselves for who we are is hard. It's hard because we spend the majority of our time either worrying about the acceptance of others or loving others without acceptance and then worrying about that.

It's an emotional battleground out there folks.

But on a serious note, self-love is very important if you want to love others. Loving yourself for who you are is the very beginning of being accepted by those who you love. If you are at odds with who you are, you cannot portray a consistent and patented version of your persona. You'll be too volatile, relationships will become stressed, manifested by you and not another. So, if you can say honestly as you read this that you like yourself, then you're doing well.

Liking yourself is a good place to be. If you have issues with your being, don't really know who you are and suffer from complexes that erode your ability for rational day to day thinking, then I'm glad you're here.

TRUST

We spoke earlier about the Universal Law of Attraction. If you vibrate on the same frequency to that which you desire, you will achieve the mastery of manifestation.

Please research a lady in the U.S named Esther Hicks. (She's more commonly known as 'Abraham Hicks'.) This lady is awesome and channels a select group of celestial spirit beings known as Abraham. They are absolute experts in the art of teaching about vibration and manifesting within your vortex here on earth. This is all carried out on stage in full view of thousands who attend her seminars.

TRUST in the Universe is a very important point. I will repeat what I have already stated and again tell you that this concept is easy to say and far harder to do.

If you and I were travelling in a car, and I told you to drive at a bridge support full on at 100 mph, explaining that just above the screaming engine you are to take your feet off the brake pedal, because the cars on-board sensors and radar will break for you... you'd have your feet hovering over that pedal for sure. I know I would. But that's what this amounts to. I'm asking you to *trust*.

Positive thoughts attract positive outcomes

Positive energy combined with a trust that all things will work out is essential if you want something badly enough. It can be almost borderline arrogance that you already know it's coming, but the key thing is to be grateful for it. Be grateful for that which you already have and not that which you think you need. Act as if life is in your favour.

Jesus was convinced without any doubt that he was going to manifest water into wine and produce fresh bread and fish that he created a miracle and altered his vibration to match that which he desired. But Jesus was an Essene, an accomplished Master and The Son of God. To everyone who was there, they called it a miracle. But he did explain that we possess the same powers, he said, 'thanks in prayer' to God.

He was truly grateful for he was about to receive.

Ring any bells? I listened to Esther Hicks once as she was channelling Abraham and they collectively told this delegate again and again the following:

"It's not about actually getting what you want. It's about the journey and enjoying the experience of the journey in allowing the vortex to create what you want. If you need to get what you want to be happy then that's not going to happen. If you trust in the experience and the journey in allowing the journey to happen in getting what you want, then the law of attraction will manifest."

There are fifty video clips on YouTube of *'Abraham Hicks'*. The Spirit Science behind it all is truly fascinating and insightful beyond comprehension. Believe me. While we're talking about getting what you want, there are other factors at play that link up with you on a daily basis without your conscious knowledge. *Abraham* will tell you that expressing what you do *not* desire in a kind of default way, tells the Universal Laws what you *do* desire, so don't be too frightened to focus on what you want. Ask ~ Focus ~ Mantra ~ Manifestation. Those are the basics. I spend all day thinking about how I want my company to succeed. That's my focus.

First thing in the morning I chant my mantra to my Spirit, and team (or anyone else who's willing to listen).

- *I am ~ grateful*
- *I am ~ successful*
- *I am ~ grateful for my wife - thank you*
- *I am ~ love and I am loved*
- *I am ~ grateful for my health*
- *I am ~ that I am*

Did you see a pattern there? *I am.*

This is Spirit Science. Those two words are the most important ones you could ever say in your thoughts or from your lips. Because whatever follows 'I AM,' is a statement to the Divine. A statement of expression and intent about who you are and a statement to God and the Universe. Remember, *what you think, so shall you become!*

THE POWER OF UNIVERSAL TRUST

"See the things that you want as already yours. Know that they will come to you at need. Then let them come. Don't fret and worry about them. Don't think about your lack of them. Think of them as yours, as belonging to you, as already in your possession."– Robert Collier

In 2014 I went on holiday with Tina and found myself laying on the beach in a sunny and beautiful paradise. Our annual vacation was always a real highlight for me, but truly essential for Tina.

Tina's career sees her managing multiple client sites and she's for the best part of the year got a mobile phone glued to her head. That in itself does bother me. The facts and findings regarding the use of microwaves near the human brain seemed to have never 'mysteriously' been offered to the public.

So, the beach... I'm not really quite sure why it came to me when it did, but it may well be the age-old cliché that being away from the woods, I could finally see the trees. What was certain was that something was beginning to stir within me, I wasn't happy until I had spilled it all out for open debate. I do remember sending this message to my dear friend Cath: *"There's a train coming and it's headed right smack bang for my station and guess what? I'm getting on it. I have no idea why or where it's going. My Spirit is screaming at me to get on that damn train because If I don't I'm going to really regret it. But it's coming alright. Soon. I'm thinking months."*

Excitedly, Tina and I both agreed I would start my own Environmental Company. Based on my experience, skill set and how much it would cost financially, it appeared outwardly to be possible. There was only one fly in the soup which would need to be confronted head on to put that final straw on the camel's back - clients. We both agreed that the cash flow to keep the company running whilst annoying, and a given, was *within acceptable limits*. I told her that I was prepared to work for her, whatever it took. The pay would be peanuts but hey, better than nothing. I remember having a focussed 'one to one' with Tina when we got back to the UK. We went over all the details again at length and I remember telling her why it was important to me that this venture works out.

"This isn't about me. I just want to put that out there. There are no hidden agendas or ulterior motives. This is about getting a company working so that firstly, I will reduce the stress associated with having to operate within a massive team of which, some ask the impossible to increase their own score line with little or no consideration for others.

I simply cannot do it any longer. So, it's about being independent and all of the gifts that managing my own time can bring. Secondly and most importantly is the end game; the bigger picture. My aim is to be able to have a company which becomes established enough to generate the maximum income required for you to be able to review your employment position. I have one wife and I know that there are no spares if you break."

So as momentum began to grow, I began to see what it was that I was up against. My focus was on building and creating. Every spare hour I would research, make lists, and prioritise. I asked Tina one question:

"Are you going to be okay with this? Are you at all scared by the prospect of me taking what some would say is a big gamble?" She explained the following:

"I'm not getting anything. I'm getting no messages. I'm not saying I know it will be fine, but I'm used to listening to my inner voice and right now, I'm not worried. I think you need to just push on. I trust you. I trust what you're doing."

I then made my statement to The Source.

"I am going to trust that the Universe will deliver me to the place which I am aiming for. I believe and trust that if I focus on my intent, the Universe has my back. It WILL work out and I am grateful for this. I say thank you for the help and Divine assistance I now call upon in order to get me where I need to be. I will succeed. This IS going to happen. I am going to trust the Universe."

I then resigned from my employed position at my former company and I think they all thought I had lost my mind. It was day 25 into my 30-day resignation period and one of my last and final jobs that would take me to my final days was at a hospital carrying out some top-up survey work. I was at an outpost building taking notes based on assets in front of me when my phone lit up.

"Hello?"
"Hi, is that Noel? Noel Hogan?"

"Yes. Who's calling please?"

"Hi Noel, it's Keith here, we met briefly last year at a site and had a chat. You were asking questions about being self-employed?

I noticed a comment recently on LinkedIn and am I correct in thinking, and please tell me to mind my own business if I'm wrong but, are you resigning?"

"You're correct Keith."

Keith then went on, *"It's just that you know I mentioned to you that I may be getting a new contract. Well, we've got it and I was wondering if you or your company would sub-contract to mine and manage it for me? Its 60 to 70 sites; It'll only take you a month or so if you plan it well. The surveys are simple enough."*

"Oh, right. Well, I'd be lying if I didn't say I was excited about that. Shall I drive down to your office next week and we can go through all of the points?"

"That'd be great Noel. The job's yours. I'll see you about nine o'clock on Tuesday then?"

"Oh yes! Cheers Keith and thank you. Thank you very much!"

I signed off and stood there; probably in complete disbelief at first. The security lady came out to see if I was alright. I told her I was fine. I looked up to the sky and just whispered *"Thank you! You never let me down!"*

Today I still sub-contract to Keith's company and we have a good working relationship. Earning the money in my first trading year gave me the financial backbone to gain all of the logistical accreditations and association fees which were required. Forming my own company has so far been a great success. It has gone better than I thought, and even allowed me to put pen to paper and write this book.

This was an element of the process which I can honestly state with clarity that I hadn't even considered when I started out. Maybe, just maybe, it's the reason WHY the Universe helped me make it happen?

I AM – that I AM.

CHAPTER EIGHT

Be the Change

"Just remember that there is a time and place for you to shine your light."

We all tend to judge others on our initial observations, but oddly enough; we don't seem to judge ourselves too readily because the judgement of others tends to be outwardly from a comparative of our own look and standards. *We* are the set standard, the benchmark *others* must measure up to. But kick that into touch and begin to accept all others without judgement and life will soon become smoother and less bumpy.

You can judge in a comparative sense. Just don't treat them according to the jury's verdict on your opinion of them as you see them. The classic is the leather clad biker, tattooed head to foot with heavy metal across his forehead. You see him walk past you and you think *"Good Lord! Please don't eat my dog!"* but then as you turn to see if he's gone, you see that he's helping an elderly or infirm person cross the road safely as no traffic would stop, so he stood in the road for them allowing safe passage.

It happens quite a lot. Don't be fooled though. It works both ways remember. The tattooed biker may well be an angel in disguise. Then there's the well-dressed man that's a regular Sunday visitor to the local church. If he walked past you, you'd think nothing but normality. Yet, nobody will tell you that he beats his wife every Friday after a session in the pub and has secret affairs. You simply have no idea about the person you see because your eyes are projectors as well as viewers and they will quite often only present the picture before you in which you wish to see.

People will not always appreciate your ideas, concepts, views and opinions. This element of life is the borderline that becomes a de-militarised zone for many. Everyone has their own beliefs and opinions to be respected or accepted. There are those who will listen readily and digest what you have to say with an open mind. They won't stamp a label on your newsfeed. They'll simply let it go in and then out and whatever interests them, will be tucked in their back pocket to play with later. That's pretty much me. *I do that*. Then there are those at the opposite end of the spectrum who, when you challenge their ideas about how everything works, will become quite angry.

This is okay, and you don't need to go any further. After all, you're not selling them your facts or beliefs but putting out the ideas and concepts. They will abandon their lower castle walls and move their artillery up to the upper castle gate called 'cognitive dissonance'. Be accepting of their anger and you're a winner. Don't inflame it, just be accepting. In the end, it's all just social mechanics.

Just remember that there's a time and place for you to shine your light. You should always be 'you'. Never feel a need to change because someone else might not like it. Never do that. Just be respectful of them and no matter their opinion of you, or what they 'think' they know about you, just remain calm and kind. You will achieve nothing by fighting fire with fire.

If you want to be the change you would like to see in others, the next time someone tries to put their opinion out there whether it is aggressive or respectful just answer with the following.

"Well that's interesting. I'll consider that. Whilst I cannot comment because it isn't a concept I'm used to, I'll certainly respect your personal viewpoint whether it's contradictory with mine or others."

What you're trying to do is not argue their view point with yours. You are effortlessly attempting to take a verbal fire extinguisher to their heated topic. And quite often, when someone is trying to impress their belief system onto you and you become immune to it by respecting their opinion, it kills the very essence and energy of it. Remember earlier in this text we concluded that not everyone is going to like you.

Some people will actively want to dislike you because it brings to the surface their own spiritual deficiencies. When you love unconditionally, as Jesus did, you will create enemies as well as admirers. You must be selective and mindful of social discourse where you can't avoid showing your metal. This is what makes us unique in a way.

You have a super power Spirit doesn't have. You can hide your true feelings and emotions. This is a key truth of being a Spirit in Spirit.

Spirits in the material world can play games. It's what we came here to experience. Spirits in Spirit cannot hide their true self. It's on display for all to see. This is why you will only reside where like-minded spirits do. You simply cannot hide your true self. So, if we're on the boat called 'change' floating down the river of opportunity a very good therapeutic action to take in these modern times which always brings controversy is **Social Media.**

Most of us use it and some of us rely on it far too much. The very best thing you could ever do is have a clear-out. I say this because it's vital that if you want to orchestrate change from within, it must start by your evaluation of the energy to mix with. You're lighting candles in a hurricane if you concentrate on your emotional state of mind daily when you are so heavily influenced by your social media news feed. So, it's always really good to have a clear out.

To be the real you, you need to keep it real. You must remain true to yourself, at all times. What we are essentially doing, but I'm not pressing on the bruise too hard here, is ensuring that you look at making your eventual return to Spirit an easier transition. Be whole, be the real you. Completed with the experiences you wanted and ready to go to the next level.

If you die *asleep*, (in a metaphoric sense) you'll have to wake up back home in Spirit and why have to do that or go through that when you can do this now? Be the genuine you, right now. No hidden agenda! No false face for the in-laws for who you haven't the time. No lies to your friends on social media just to keep them from getting upset. If you want to change, moving forward there will be waves.

I think if you were a smoker or a drinker, gambler, and you know what it's like to quit, then this really is no different. You will lose (what you thought were) friends on the way and your habitual thinking will have to be cultivated in new soil. I'm sure you know what I mean, the friends who you probably only see at weddings or once a year when they come around to catch up on gossip (and then get your current situation and go and gossip about you ~ adding value to make it more interesting). These are the 'hangers on' which have to go. Start there and move outward. Especially with those that cannot be bothered to come and see you but want to know exactly what you're up to by checking out your profile.

These aren't friends. You don't need them. They will more than likely be the very people who delight in negative gossip and fill your news feed with rubbish and negative thinking. Visualise placing them in an emotional wicker basket and pushing them gently out to sea with love and kindness. No nastiness. No resentment. No hate or regret. Just say your farewell with love and simply move on. Your relationship with them is now over.

In a nut shell, you realised that they add no value to your existence and what there is, is not conducive to your positive outlook on life. Let them go.

YOUR VIBE WILL ATTRACT YOUR TRIBE

If you like to be with others who walk down the street, pointing fingers, calling other's names and bullying, if you want to try and impress them into accepting you, you will soon learn to think as they do. Thoughts are energy. Energy is a life force. What you think ~ you shall become.

However, should you seek solace with spiritually minded souls who only want to seek kindness and search out life in accordance with love and empathy, and want the best for others, you make a positive transition toward revealing who you really are. How can I impress upon you the significance of change beginning with you? On the following page is a checklist to remind yourself on a daily basis that you are on your way to becoming the ultimate and real you.

At the end of this book I have listed similar points as mantras. When read weekly these will remind you about why you should follow them in order to stay focussed on being the real you.

- I am - that I am
- I am grateful
- I am blessed
- I am love and I am loved
- My thoughts are energy
- What I think ~ I become
- What I think ~ I attract
- I am not defined by my past
- I will accept all others regardless of colour – race - religion and sexuality
- I make my enemies my friends the day I forgive them
- I will not judge others but embrace their viewpoint as an aspect of who they are and not who I am
- I will find the positive within the negative in every event
- I will aim to protect myself from negative energy
- I must aim to walk away from negative energy and people who attack my being
- I will look out for signs from my Spirit because I trust in my Spirit's presence
- I will trust the Universe to join the dots ahead of me - it has my back
- I believe in myself
- I want to be the best version of me I can
- I do not regret what I have done in my life this far - it has helped shape who I have become
- I will not set limitations on myself
- I can - I will

CHAPTER NINE

Happiness is an Inside Job

"To stay in your comfort zone teaches you nothing and just serves to massage your ego."

One of the most vital aspects of how you view this life is this: you might have problems, but nobody has it easy. Quite often everyone you see or meet is having issues and struggling on a daily basis. The millionaire has probably more problems and daily stresses to deal with than you or I combined, but here's the thing. We often mistake wealth for contentment. Not so. Happiness actually comes from within. It has absolutely nothing to do with what we attach ourselves to materially.

Happiness is a state of consciousness, a state of mind; a choice. A subsequent result of the decisions and choices you make in life. There are some people that have been sucked into the media adverts and glossy 'chat' magazine articles who consider themselves less than worthy to be seen in public because they haven't achieved wealth. Not only this, but they worry their 'so called' friends will judge them due to their style choices and the fact that they haven't got the latest fashions. Some people live day to day having plastic bits tucked under their skin to enhance their looks and poison injected into their faces. I wish people could really see that whole fraud for what it is. It's a commercial fraud and what's more it destroys people's spirit. It's all about companies making millions from human insecurity. Remember, where there's a need, there's greed.

I have no time for any of it. However, I will treat those people with the kindness and respect with which I would like to be treated. We're not here to enjoy being the ultimate success stories of ourselves on a continual self-absorbed back patting competition. Nobody learns by hanging out with just the 'winners'. But I do say that I either win, or I learn. There's no losing and one particular day I was reminded of this great lesson.

I played squash with a good friend of mine on a regular basis during my former RAF days and I think it's fair to say that day to day, it was like ping pong. One day, Mat would win; the next I would, and so on and so forth. One day, he was on leave and I was itching to get down to the courts but didn't know anyone else who played. So, I took my racket and just went down to vent some energy, smack the ball around and sweat off my 'itch' and try some racket techniques with off-spin etc. I walked through the door to the court and low and behold, there was another friend, Taff. What on earth was he doing here? I had no idea he played.

Due to squadron shifts he was usually at work when I went to the courts with Mat. So, he just politely asked me if I wanted a match. *"Be rude not to,"* I thought to myself. That was probably the dumbest thing I ever did. Nobody had the chance to warn me that he played for the Station Team and periodically sat on the Ivory Throne with the golden racket on the Station Leader Board. I suffered complete humiliation and defeat beyond measure.

Taff assured me that despite me losing most spectacularly, I was in fact getting better as I went on and he told me there were periods during the game where he felt he was being tested.

He played the best he could but every now and then I'd have him on the run. This humiliation of mine went on for about four evenings and despite never winning a match, I did feel better for it. Mat came back from leave the next week and we went down to play. I kicked his ass that badly; something like an all-out total whitewash, that he ignored me for about five days. But the point here is this. You have to walk with those greater, to learn to be a 'master' yourself.

To stay in your comfort zone and keep playing competitors you know you can beat, teaches you nothing and just serves to massage your ego. Not a Spiritual lesson but a *life lesson* with a shadow of Spiritual essence about it.

In life, you are learning to condition yourself to be the best version of you that you can. It will feel at times as though it's a battlefield, because you'll be tested again and again.

Being beaten at squash then beating Mat was never about the test. It was simply how I reacted to the losing and then the winning. I was gracious in defeat and thanked Taff for teaching me. I told Mat that it was due to his lack of practice that I'd beaten him, not because I'd upped my skill level playing someone better.

I'm not quite sure about the concept of Karma. I don't fully buy into the idea about lessons being learned and repeatedly returning until they are so, Or, I'm missing something very important and *it is in fact very much the case*. But there has to be some sort of schedule for us if we can agree that we chose to come here, and it is all planned out and pre-managed in the 'celestial office'. I know there are no coincidences.

Your life is very much on purpose. There is within your circles and for the benefit of all, a 'divine plan' at work.

ANGER

Who doesn't get angry? Who doesn't feel a bit better launching a few teddies out from the cot now and then? Even Jesus, the Teacher of Love got angry in the temples. It is one of the most fundamental basic emotional responses that we have in our personal tool box and on occasions extremely necessary for our survival. So, if you want to be more spiritual, should you learn not to be angry? *(While we're at it, is that actually possible?)*

I'm not a fully qualified counsellor but, I can explain in a clear unscientific manner why in my opinion, it's quite okay to be angry. It's very much about the next phase in your thinking and how you channel your anger which is what learning to become more spiritual is actually about.

Let's look at one hypothetical example then:

I'm away on an appointment and call my wife. *"I'll be home for 5pm all being well with traffic. We'll leave for the ferry port and hopefully be in Northern Ireland for midnight. Okay darling, see you soon. Love you."*

Departing the office, as I turn onto the motorway I notice a strange sound and quickly decide to pull over. A nail has gone through the tyre and it's right on the wall so, not repairable. It's a tyre change.

No problem, the spare tyre is under the back. Luckily I've unknowingly pulled over in a safe spot but the wheel won't come off because the retaining butterfly flange has been damaged. The car must have driven over a speed bump too fast at some point and the result is a broken stud. Marvellous!

After a quick call back to the office a colleague arrives and with *'percussion precision'* the wheel is freed and swapped. I am back in the game losing only 20 minutes. Then Tina calls, luckily I'm on hands-free Bluetooth.

"Where are you? You should have been here by now?"

"Sorry babe, I got a flat tyre and had to get help because the spare was jammed."

"You know if we're held up any more, we've no time in the Bank. We will miss our boat!"

"I know. Please don't state the obvious? You think I 'wanted' to get my suit all dirty and oh, oh great...."

"Oh great .... What?"

"I'm coming to a stop. There must have been a crash or a breakdown? Brilliant. Well, that's it then. Abort the ferry. No chance now. I just cannot see another way around the M62 from here?"

"Why don't you leave earlier next time? I did warn you!"

"Oh right. So, it's my entire fault now? You decided not to take yesterday off when we 'could' have gone when these roads would have been quiet! Tina ~ Tina? Are you there?"

The phone goes dead and Tina has refused to argue.

I'm seething. I have all the rest of the time and length of the three remaining motorways and forty-five minutes to boil over. When I arrive home there's a negative fog of energy in the house.

Bags are unpacked. The TV goes on and there are grumpy faces all round.

"Tonight, on Channel 4 news - PASSENGERS IN HELL... The daring escape captured on camera by a motorist as a ferry from Cairn Ryan to Belfast smashes into the harbour wall and catches fire. There is only thought to be five survivors due to the fire being out of reach of rescue workers."

I look at Tina. Tina looks at me and we just hug. We both say "I'm so sorry. That could have been us. Oh, my Lord. Thank goodness you got that flat tyre. *I guess someone upstairs was looking out for us?"*

So yes, I got angry a little and so did Tina. Frustration will always knock on the door first and usually morph into anger but that's as far as we try and let it go. Containment is the lesson we are trying to teach ourselves not a fight or flight outburst. It didn't come out of control and bitterness.

This is where adults are quite good at becoming children again, as you see your argument slipping away you turn your attention to finger pointing and personal insults. This example showed us how a negative situation turned out to be a very positive one for us, but sadly not for others, which can be quite common. A very big lesson was learned.

Staying angry achieves very little and I think we can all agree that it won't be too long until our thoughts are interrupted enough for that anger to subside.

But the key to it all is to somehow prevent your personal anger or frustration from crashing someone else's party. This is how the 'ripple in the pond' effect works and within both areas of positive and negative actions.

It's my belief that nearly all scenarios we find ourselves in are for the greater good. Even if at the time you think otherwise. During our lives we must be prepared for the fact that those who silently protect us and guide us, will do whatever it takes to keep us heading in the right direction. It may mean ensuring that you fail that job interview. At the time you walked out thinking it's a done-deal, only to then receive a very thin envelope from the employer with a single sheet of headed A4 stating:

"Thank you for your interest in our company. Sadly, on this occasion you were unsuccessful, however in the future this may change. We will keep your records on our file. Regards the CEO."

Two months later and the job of your entire lifetime lands on your lap without so much as a sniff and you're thinking *"Gee, I wonder if not getting that other job was actually a blessing in disguise?"*

There are plenty of blessings, but *never coincidences.* Things that seem to randomly happen and far beyond any comprehension when you try and imagine the logistics of how some 'supreme celestial being' has orchestrated it all. It just isn't possible not even for the most powerful computer to manage. But that should give you an idea of just how powerful *you* are. Because along with some of your soul family, *you* did indeed arrange it all So getting angry about *'he said'* and *'she said'* and the *'world's so cruel'* and life's just so unfair seems a bit ridiculous.

In 1998, Irish-American author Malachy McCourt was quoted as saying, *"I had a murderous rage in my heart of Limerick, the humiliation of coming out of the slums,"* he says of his hometown in Ireland, the setting of his brother Frank McCourt's Pulitzer Prize-winning memoir, *"Angela's Ashes."*

"It made you feel like nothing and there was no place to go but down. It was assumed we'd be low-class the rest of our lives. But who can you blame? Governments and churches which are gone now?

It's useless. Let those things live rent-free in your head and you'll be a lunatic. Resentment is like taking poison and waiting for the other person to die."

When you are bitter and resentful about another, they own you. They're in your thinking and shackled to your daily routine weighing you down. It is true when you stop to think about it. So, the only thing you need to do is find it in yourself to forgive them, let it go, and move on. They exit your consciousness stage left. No more rent-free lodging in your space.

You cannot afford to give others that allowance if you are to improve your life. You must let them go. Forgive them. Not because they deserve your forgiveness but because you deserve the emotional unattached freedom to their negative energy.

There are many ways in which people deal with their anger. It's what suits you best, but once you forgive your enemies, you make them your friends even if you never communicate with or see them again. You cannot be stressed due to their actions and you cannot be stressed by their words anymore because they are not your enemy. They are no longer part of your daily thought process.

This whole forgiveness thing may sound a little *out there,* but you can study all manner of situations and find a good reasoning for it when you take a forensic look at your daily lives.

Take for example your drive to work. How many times has someone raced along your nearside and then cut in front of you or (my real pet-hate) sped past you at warp speed only to pull across in front of you braking, 'making you brake' to take the exit when, they could have just slowed down behind you and pulled off. How annoying and dangerous? The trick though, is to summon the whole strength of your positivity power and say The Self-Repair Exercise.

"Okay. I see. But one day you'll do that to the wrong person. I however, am the right person. I'm your lucky day because I actually haven't got the spare energy to waste on this act of complete stupidity and inconsiderate irresponsible madness. So, have a nice day. Please drive more safely and with courtesy for other road users in future."

Whilst that was a long and complete statement, when a few well-placed expletives or a recognised British traffic hand signal would suffice, you'll notice there's good reason for that and when you actually try it you'll discover something. It isn't possible to stay angry for any length of time once you've fooled yourself into taking another alternate train of thought. It's like if you broke into song. You simply couldn't stay angry. What there was would be doused with normality, and rage extinguished with kindness and understanding.

You've made a judgement about them: "What a total knucklehead." Your treatment of them upon your judgement was, "I hope you have a nice (safe) day, for the benefit of everyone!" This self-repair exercise is definitely worth trying the next time some knucklehead annoys you.

But on a serious note here, it does train you to deal with daily testing situations which directly feed your ego and your judgement. You are now in the business of rebuilding your cognitive auto-response. Anger is a release based on your perceptions. You don't need it, as it serves no purpose. Let it go. Believe me and trust me, it does work.

See the things that you want as already yours

What you reap – you will sow...

You are out shopping with your wife and you pop into a local store. Sitting across the road is a homeless person with the usual traits, cardboard sign, maybe a dog with him. He looks very skinny and bedraggled. You decide that you can find it in you to approach this person and hand them some money. You want to make it okay, even if it's just for today. You reach into your wallet and put it back into your pocket, because there's only bank notes in there and you need to find 'spare change'.

Hang on! What did you learn from reading this book? So, you pick back up the change and reach for the five pound note you saw in your wallet. Excellent, you feel good about yourself and they have some cash to get some food or buy some cigarettes.

Oh, and by the way, what's wrong with that? Do you want to help them or be their health guru as well? It's about you giving them the freedom to choose what they want from their needs. They have asked for them by sitting there. But every action has an equal and opposite reaction does it not? The Laws of the Universe state *"What you reap, you shall sow." "What you give out, shall return to you in more measure."*

A true example of this in action came about quite recently. My wife had given a similar chap a £10 note and when she popped into the store she bought a Lottery Scratch Card to give him too as she came out the other side, but he'd moved on.

Disappointed she got back into her car and began to drink her coffee, only to scratch the card and yes, you guessed it. She won £20. So for Tina her measure and level of response was immediate.

Please take note though. To give to others with the express expectation that you'll somehow hopefully gain simply won't work. There's no Spiritual Stock Market or Craps Table. You cannot give a homeless person a £20 note and think £40 is coming your way. That's not how life's script is written I'm afraid.

HAPPINESS

Success is everything. Money means success. A bigger house is better. A more expensive car tells people that you're a winner at life. *What complete and utter bunkum.* Firstly, you need to forget what society says and decide for yourself. Define what success means to you? How do you feel about the term success and what is your definition of it?

It actually all boils down to what makes you happy coupled with not caring what others think of you, those two things and nothing more. Remember we spoke about having to accept a concept? Not caring about other peoples' opinions of you because it's none of your business? Well, once you've mastered that, you're free. Once you're free, you can be anything you want; anything that makes you happy. Happiness is the real success in this life.

There are plenty of billionaires buried in the graveyard who I bet regret some of their life choices. Not so much the money, but how they managed it.

But whilst we're talking about the super-rich here's a point to ponder. Do those who get rich want to get rich so that they are happy, or so that other people will admire them with their expensive and elaborate cars and boats which then in turn makes them feel better about themselves? You decide.

I watched a documentary about a man who I quite respected because he was deconstructing his personality during a documentary. "So, what the hell am I doing here? Why am I so unhappy with this? I need to change?" He had amassed a fortune through his very good skill and judgement, but the negative side was, whilst being seen to invest wisely in property all over the globe, he then complained to the camera that he had to employ managers to manage the managers of his estates.

He didn't mind forking out two hundred million for a beautiful mansion by the lake in Italy, it was the massive expense and headache of having to maintain it and above all, trust his managers. Which in select areas, he didn't. Running multi-national estates was making him very unhappy.

- If you ask a Salmon what the meaning of success is, it will tell you in fish speak that it's about swimming back to the still waters of it's birth place, to breed and spawn. Often tens of thousands of river miles just swimming.

- Ask a tree. The tree will just explain that success is living. Being a tree. It doesn't look at other trees and feel threatened or insecure. It just gets on with being a tree. No matter the branches or shape, a beautiful tree.

- Look up in the sky and observe the clouds. Do you ever see a wrong cloud?

- Observe the stunning diversity of the ocean waves; all of them different but none of them wrongly fashioned.

So, ask a person what their concept of happiness is, and the answer can be totally impossible to guess. We, unlike our natural wildlife who just get on with it, have others within our flock who live for the benefits that extreme wealth can bring and whether or not you like it, you have been recruited to assist in that.

You have your life to do with as you see fit, but you also have this shadow life attached to you cooperating and conforming to rules and bowing to ideas about how that life of yours should be lived.

You're living for society, the rich. The elite, helping them amass their billions and secondly, a part time job ~ scraping a living until now that is. If you've got your big boy pants on, we'll look at your new thinking because I'm willing to guess that something's clicked and you just decided 'enough'; enough of this phoney illusion already.

"It's time to change who I am. I am no longer the person that society wants me to remain. I am not defined by my past or the mistakes I have made."

You can achieve anything you want. You will be a success because, you now know that success is 'being' the real you. Life is the success. Memories will always slay materialism. Happiness is found within a walk by the river and not inside a leather wallet. Success is being real; being you. The ultimate real *you* that you were looking for and now, you've realised that all along you were right here and all you have to do is switch you off, and then back on again.

- *Money is an illusion of the great. It is the ghost of success.*
- *Nobody on this Earth is any better or any worse a person than anyone else.*
- *We are all connected. We're just all walking different chosen paths.*
- *Conformity is the jailer of freedom and the enemy of personal growth.*

Have a cognitive defrag. All you have to do is change your thinking. The new you is imminent. Because as far as thinking goes, it's 'out with the old and in with the new'. You're going to be a success now because you understand life and Spiritual Science. Be thankful for it. It's about trusting the journey towards it, not the arrival.

WHAT I THINK – I BECOME

You are going to succeed in your new life because you are going to learn to forgive those who wrong you. You're going to find it within your core being to say;

"I'm done being bitter. I'm done being angry at you. I'm forgiving you and placing you in a beautiful boat and casting you off to sea with love. We shall meet again and when we do, it'll all be okay, because I don't have to die and pass across to my home in Spirit to put this all straight. I'm correcting it this second. You're okay. You're my friend. I am going to call on my own guide, my own Spirit to understand that I acknowledge its presence in my daily life and I know and trust that it is very much there."

You may not be able to see your Spirit, but I know from my own experience that it loves you and wants the very best for you. Your Spirit has been on this journey many thousands of times, so trust it. Your Soul is eternal, listen where you can to create stillness in your mind; with stillness comes calm and these are the tools for learning to feel your journey more. You are more than your experiences, more than your body. You are eternal, a gift to yourself and others 'I am - that I am'. You are going to learn to trust your feelings and not rely so much on what you are told; what you see.

Switch on and trust your Spiritual Sat Nav and feel your way. Above all else, when the questions are answered call on your own Spirit and ask:

"Does this feel right?"

Remember that Rome wasn't built in a day so don't spend your entire life searching for more answers than you can ask questions. Life is a gift worthy of experiencing and living. We all too often forget that we are gifted this one true chance to shine our light and experience this earth in all her majesty.

The next time you are given a gift of life you will be someone else, so here and now and being you will only happen once in Eternity. Wow! Just think about that for a second. In the end, and I constantly tell myself this, you'll eventually arrive back in Spirit to probably regret spending so much time searching for life answers. You may well discover that the life you spent trying to piece together, all the clues to big questions, will be superseded by one gigantic Encyclopaedia of the Universe upon landing back in the celestial heavens. Don't waste too much time getting bogged down with how the fireworks are made, just enjoy the display.

To continue, we all need to find out as much as we can about ourselves in order to be able to then relax and kick back. It's important to find out about the big stuff; the nuts and bolts of life and where we came from and eventually travel to. Why we are here; who we are and perhaps even why we came here. These are all the big bits. The questions about black holes and where the Universe ends, is best left to those who have spent a lifetime enjoying that ride!

So, there you go. The next time you venture out of your house - think differently.

Tell the Universe just how beautiful the sky looks, how the song of the dawn chorus was a melody to behold and not an annoying noise. Acknowledge that you appreciate life for the gift that has been given to you to use whilst you are here. And last but not least, be mindful of your thoughts minute by minute for they are also a conversation with the Universe.

You now know that what you think; you create and attract. So, think good things. Help others and forgive yourself for your troubled past along with those who you once considered your enemies. On this gift of a journey through life, when you are presented with a situation to navigate just remember what we discussed here in this little book you read.

Don't get too bogged down in what you're told or what your eyes see. Let your own being tell you how it feels. Learning to trust your own Sat Nav is the answer. It will serve you well. Life will get a whole lot better. It's going to be okay. Everything will work out right in the end.

If it isn't right ... well, it's not the end!

CHAPTER TEN

A Daily Script

"You have the power to actually heal yourself."

You must never think of yourself as limited or restricted. Based on what we've covered within the writings of this book, you'll now understand the significance of how a negative thought process can undermine your ability to achieve that which you seek. But what about that which you are - flesh and blood? How does negative thinking affect the human body?

To begin with, let us go back to that statement:

'What you think – you attract'.

If you now think *'you don't feel well,'* the Universe (without being personally vindictive) will answer you back. We're saying here that you are *stating* that you don't feel well. Actually, it's more than likely quite justified. Something really doesn't feel right. People do have aches and pains. Be mindful of negative states of sickness though. Those states of accepting that you're always going to be ill, almost convincing yourself of being ill even if at the moment, you're not.

There are those who 'want to be ill' as it gives them attention from others. It's a statement of who they are. *"Oh, I'm always* coming down with something!" and so, you almost give in to this preconceived understanding. You mustn't ever accept that as a concept. You can control everything that comes at you from either a cognitive angle or a physical one. The most important aspect of this though is how you respond to those pains. You call the shots remember. You decide whether they stay or go:

A DAILY SCRIPT:

You: "I'm sick."

The Universe: *"Yes, you are. Here you are - have more sickness. You can thank me later."*

You: "I wish I was well."

The Universe: *"By saying you wish is implying you are not accepting you already are, and only hoping to be. You keep telling me this and it's my job to make sure you have all you need in this life. You just have to decide with your free will just what it is."*

You: "Why, is this always happening to *me*?"

The Universe: *"It's happening because you make the statement of your intent. Haven't you been reading this book?"*

You: "Oh, this is rubbish. I'm sick. Why always me? I just feel like I want to die...."

The Universe: *"Ahem!!!.... Excuse me. I really wouldn't go there if I were you!"*

The first concept of Spirit Science is to plant the seed of *The Law of Attraction* firmly. Nourish it, and allow it to grow in positivity. Understand though, that like a flower, it will take time and patience. The moment you have this thinking under your control, you begin to reap the harvest born of the seeds of positivity and that's a very good thing. Not just for you, but for everyone you connect and interact with. The ripple effect of positive energy will reach friends and acquaintances as it has a knock-on effect. Your body though, is a miracle all on its own. What I'm about to tell you may come as a bit of a shock - however, trust me on this.

You, have the power to heal yourself.

You can reverse the damage of illness, and repair your body by pure thought alone. Think about it. If being negative can increase disease and cause illness, then positive thoughts about you and a focus on self-love and self-healing will actually reverse the process.

Jesus the teacher of Love was particularly proficient at this.

You are actually a God - not the God - but a God of millions of cells in your whole body. You are their leader, their boss, their mentor. You guide them and instruct them. You feed them. You are their God. However, you can also be their Devil.

If you understand this, then understand that what you think has a direct influence on not only what you attract, but also, what you become from within. If you play the victim on a day to day basis, you will never fully feel totally vibrant and well. This in turn has a knock-on effect in that you will not attract a good experience outwardly.

You will live an existence of pure survival, and the important thing to remember, is that it's going to be moderately okay to deal with when you're young, which is a relatively brief period of your life. The clock of human invention is ticking remember, and your body is moving along the track of 'tick ~ tock'. Time is not ticking, *you are*. You tick, with every cell that dies and becomes replaced with revitalised ones.

Like the sun, you have a finite resource of energy called 'body cells' and there are only so many to go around. This is real life. Not time in years. Cell life. How long it takes for you to use up all of your cells through regeneration until one day, the majority of the areas and organs of what was once a youthful group of cells, has become slower, more tired, and less responsive. This then looks toward an inevitable tipping point where cell regeneration cannot sustain itself.

Your body hears everything your mind says.

Moving forward from today, I cannot stress how important that statement is. If you are the God to the living cells within you, like our Divine God that created all, you must learn to love your body cells. Above all else though, you must *want to love them.'* In turn, this will lead you to ultimately love yourself. This is what we are really talking about when we talk of *'loving the self.'* Now, covering the mind, or consciousness, there exists a 'two-pronged' attack on your body. It is attacked by you on a daily basis. Whilst your cells are networking and being magnificent team players to bring about the success of the working, living, human body, if you're not careful you're putting flies in the ointment on two basic fronts.

- Firstly, what you think. If you think and submit to pain and discomfort, then you will give the signal to the Universe that you're hungry for more. Not necessarily more of the same right now, because manifestation takes a little time. No, just when that ill feeling has eased because you've begun to relax, and your train of thought distracted from it, in about a day or so you will have something else to moan about.

- Secondly, whilst you're pacing up and down outside in the cold air because you don't want to smoke in the house as it smells ... well, let's stop right there. Just look at that. You smoke. It's not a thought this time but a physical action. Second hand smoke is the combination of smoke from the burning end of a cigarette and the smoke breathed out by smokers. Second hand smoke contains more than 7,000 chemicals which are toxic and can cause cancer.

"You burn toxins in a rolled-up bit of paper and breathe it in, creating a layer of tar on the organs which you need, which you absolutely depend on, for your very survival? Excuse me? ... You do this for 'enjoyment?' Have you completely lost your mind?" Who told you this was a good idea?

Millions do it. But they are at war with their health. It was born of an addiction and now the mind and body are at odds in a vicious never-ending circle. If your body had a voice, I can tell you that you're about to get some grief and it isn't going to be pretty!

Then there's drink. One glass of red wine is apparently good for you. But that's one. If you were like me in the eighties, you fill your body with poisons and toxins. I used to do it excessively. Five days a week. You do this until it overcomes the bloodstream and ends up diffusing and altering the electrical grid of your operating system?

People have said drinking is worse than smoking. Hmm... my argument is that smoking leaves a deposit within your body whilst altering your chemical balance.

Drinking takes something away whilst altering your body's chemical balance. But drinking at the other end of the spectrum is a habit that can destroy those lives around you as well as yours.

Then there's food. You know that all the food you eat from that fast food outlet isn't real food, right? There's no real goodness in it. It's designed to keep you dependent on it. It won't affect everyone but that's not the end game.

'Monosodium Glutamate' MSG for short, is the salt form of glutamic acid, which is a naturally occurring amino acid. MSG produces a savoury but salty taste when added to food, which excites your taste buds and stimulates the release of brain chemicals called neurotransmitters, then Bingo! Depending on your resistance to it and your state of mind, you can become addicted to it. As many do. So the downward spiral commences. You eat far too much of one particular food substance and your body looks about to see where it can store all the excess fats, which are specifically introduced to the food to make it 'taste good.'

It ends up round the waist and stomach and you become fat. An increase in body size will ultimately slow you down and make you less active. Being less active reduces the endorphins created within your chemical body that set the conditions for happiness and mood. This makes you more susceptible to conditions like Diabetes and all manner of other ailments causing you to be depressed.

Then just as you're feeling depressed you catch yourself in the mirror and now you're *really* depressed. This leads you to ultimately begin to hate who you are. This is the point of no return for many. It isn't impossible to turn this around by any means, but the struggle to get back to personal happiness is a very large mountain to climb, and will often require the assistance of gifted, loving angelic souls who are here to get you back on track.

There is a serious message here. That message is love your body. Love the cells which go to make up who you are. Treat them kindly and forgive them. The next time you feel an ache or a pain, pause. Think about what I've said. Then take five deep breaths in through the nose and slowly out through the mouth.

Read this following statement of intent to your body. *Yes*, you'll probably think it's time for the men in white coats but that's okay. This is something you're not used to. Just like looking back at yourself in the mirror and telling yourself, "I love you." It's a bit odd. It's actually quite hard.

"My dear body cells, I love you all individually and collectively. Thank you for putting up with my moods and my negativity. As of this moment, the tide has turned. As of today, the fightback begins. I am going to love you guys more and acknowledge and appreciate everything that you do, to go toward making me who I am.

I acknowledge and appreciate your daily struggle to keep me alive and healthy, despite my poor life choices.

I am well in mind, body and spirit. I thank you for being a part of, and collectively, a whole of who I am"

Let's talk about the ethos of this book subject, shall we?

THINKING – YOUR MIND

Now this is where it can start to become geeky and complicated when you begin to study the entire concept of what thought is, where it comes from, and the resulting accounts of those who have physically died in body and travelled to spirit. Scientists are at odds on a day to day basis when offering their views and professional opinions about the human brain which tickles me pink I have to say.

Please don't think I'm disrespecting them because I have no intention; far from it. They are super humans who do great things, quite often saving precious lives and I have nothing but admiration and respect. But here's where I start to scratch my head. I have an issue with the constant argument that when the brain dies (starved of blood oxygen) the human body *cannot* come back to life and function in a way in which it did prior to death.

Many thousands of human beings have been declared dead for over an hour with pulse oximeters registering nothing, only to come back to life and recover fully hours later in the morgue, and furthermore, to write an intelligent and thorough account of their 'alternative experience.' The hilarious element to this whole argument being, that these people were still functioning and feeling, expressing emotions and digesting information, far more powerfully than when they were back in their bodies?

Their vision, awareness, capability and knowledge amongst other things had taken on that of a comic book super hero. They would explain that their senses were more heightened than ever. Yet, given this fascinating research material taken from many thousands of individuals, some scientists still argue that all emotion and thought is derived from that mushy squidgy walnut that's suspended in fluid within your skull – your brain!

THE FERRARI THEORY:

The brain is a miracle in itself. Let's just be clear about that. It is yet to be fully mapped and has the complexity of a small Universe about it. It is truly magnificent.

I believe that the brain's main function is to read data via electrical signals in order to drive the body. It simply controls function which, again, is quite a marvel when you look at how muscles work. The perfect analogy for me is this: Take a modern Ferrari. Expensive, beautiful, crafted to perfection. A gift! You are the Ferrari in separate entities.

Stay with me on this...

- The car body is your body. Arms, legs, head, feet etc.
- The car engine is your brain. Responsible for power, drive, generating electrical energy from the alternator.
- The car driver is your consciousness. *Not your mind. Or your brain.* Just your consciousness.

Your consciousness is the driver. The Ferrari is your body. The engine of the car is your brain which is physical and made of matter. The engine ensures that all the signals and power are sent to all the areas that are required for the car to move.

When you stop the car and get out, you are asleep. Once you get back in the car, you are awake. The brain is connected to the body via the consciousness. Once you get back out of the car it's night time again and you, the driver, switch to a mode without the car called sub-consciousness. That's dream state and all other manner of journeys but without the physical car - your body.

What our surgeon friends are stating then is - that once the engine fails and throws a piston, the car is in trouble and will miss-fire until it either stops or detonates.

What about the driver though? (What we have agreed is consciousness) He can just climb out. Walk away. Maybe come back down the road another day in another different car - maybe a Lamborghini?

Have you understood what I've tried to explain there?

Brain function is the Operations Centre, the life force of necessity for the human body to function along with the heart however, when we talk about Mind, Body, Spirit, I am tempted to suggest that not all of your thinking can come from your brain. I'm suggesting it is coming from your consciousness, just like The Cloud where you store all that extra music and files on your tablet.

Okay then, let's go back and look at our car (Body) for another example.

You get in your Ferrari and on your journey, just like we've already suggested, something goes wrong with the engine (Your brain). If the engine cannot be repaired, the car will not appear to run as it should. However, what a lot of people see, is a car whose life is damaged and not able to function correctly. It doesn't drive normally.

So what have we explained about the driver - anything?

No. The driver is perfectly healthy and intact. It's just the car engine. So, whilst we turn that car into our human body, people will see characteristics which would give a clue as to the engine problems. Signals aren't being sent from the brain to arms and leg muscles as they once were, maybe even facial muscles? Those people however have a driver in their seat called consciousness, and they are fully aware and every bit as intelligent as you or me; some, more so.

I draw upon the example of the magnificent human being named Dr Stephen Hawking CH CBE FRS FRSA a Theoretical Physicist, Cosmologist and Author as an example. So, when you see a wheelchair bound person, just recall what we know here.

I have always come to the conclusion that we are holographic representations of who we are in Spirit. The physical appearance would differ upon each new life experience because think about it, your features are the combination of your parents' DNA. Unless this was replicated in Spirit time and time again, it's hard to imagine you looking identical once crossed back into the spirit realm as that which you did on Earth.

In truth, you've more than likely experienced infinite experiences as a human or 'another' alternate intelligent life form. That in itself is a really nuts concept to try and get your head around and one which I was stupid enough to bring up with one of my family members.

The conversation went thus:

"So, Noel, tell me, do you believe that we are not alone?"

"No. *We're not.*"

"How can you prove that?"

"Mum's just through there in the kitchen."

"Yes, hilarious. You know what I was trying to ask."

"No Dad. We're not alone. To begin with, let's study the findings of the Deep Field HST (Hubble Space Telescope) survey shall we? Now you know I'm a NASA geek and anything paranormal or extra-terrestrial gets my attention. But the Deep Field Experiment was a real wide eye opener for the astrological and astronomic communities."

The idea for the Hubble Deep Fields project originated after examining the exposures from the initial fix of the lenses taken after the space mission to repair it in 1993. The new more recent images revealed a surprising quantity of galaxies, which were often quite different from those we see in the local Universe and could not otherwise be studied using conventional ground-based powerful telescopes.

The first Deep Field survey, the Hubble Deep Field North (HDF-N), was observed over 10 consecutive days during Christmas 1995. The resulting image consisted of 342 separate exposures, with a total exposure time of more than 100 hours, compared with typically routine Hubble exposures of a few hours. The surveyed region of sky in Ursa Major was carefully selected to be as empty as possible so that Hubble would look far beyond the stars of our own Milky Way and out past nearby galaxies.

The results were stunning! A count of nearly three thousand galaxies were identified and confirmed in the image.

Scientists analysed the images statistically and found that the HDF had seen back to the very young Universe where the bulk of the galaxies had not, as yet, had time to form stars. Or, as the popular press dramatically reported,

"Hubble sees back to *Big Bang*!"

"So then Dad; given that there are more stars in our immediate galaxy than there are grains of sand in all Earth's beaches (so it is said), taking into consideration then that in one tiny section of the sky, the Deep Field Survey revealed approximately three thousand galaxies, and they have millions of billions of stars which have solar systems all around them, you're still saying that Earth is it! That we, are the only ones and there's nobody else out there?"

"Yes."

"Wow! Got to say, if that isn't the most arrogant of perceptions within the entirety of the human species Dad, then I don't know what is?"

I left that day with a deep sense of disappointment that my own father had such a deep routed hard-core faith in the Bible and his religion, that he couldn't even consider life in other worlds, or anything which he felt contradicted his understanding. This was a great shame. After all, I never once said he had to give up his belief system. Never once did I suggest that he should *change* his belief in *his* religion. I just hinted that it might benefit his future experiences to be more open minded.

Add to the value of what he already understands; why not play with the idea that there may well be other life, on other planets?

By the way, if you think that human beings are the only species of life in the entire known Universe I don't have a problem with that. (But I will suggest you might be in for a little surprise one day in the future...)

As we go about our lives today, it is now beginning to appear what a few of us have suspected all along has in fact been the case and there is a major government cover-up. To what extent, and to what end, regarding the interaction with what species of alternative life form is still tantalisingly out of reach. However, there are suggestions that there is and have been for some time, other species of human here on earth; apparently arriving here during the Second World War from a galaxy only forty-five minutes away in their reality and travel time.

Mind boggling fascinating stuff when you begin to dig for answers, it's utter 'tosh' to many though and that's really okay. I've watched footage of military missiles being 'shot down' and disabled with what outwardly appears to be *light beams* online. Very genuine and not tampered with or staged hoaxes as most are, and testimony statements from extremely credible sources whom, in the Autumn of their last days have decided to spill the truth for the sake of mankind. Why would they lie? What do they have to gain apart from maybe some extremely sick prank?

One particular scientist from America talked about a known underground base where *'they'* arrive and depart. He showed old Polaroid slides taken in the 70s of his liaison with friendly ETs he worked alongside. Their crafts are of something straight out of Star Trek, and they informed their hosts on Earth that they are here to observe and try and prevent us from destroying the planet.

Now then, decide what you will about the possibility of aliens, green bogey men, tall white stick beings with big eyes etc. however, this is where I begin to see an element of this whole E.T thing for a logical truth and how plausible it could be, in Spirit Circles.

It is well documented that those who have travelled back to Spirit only to be sent back here, have explained time and time again the same truth.

The Universe was watching. The Universe was listening. I asked the Universe for emergency assistance...

CHAPTER ELEVEN

Invisible Assistance

"Just because you cannot see them, doesn't mean they're not there."

During 1998 I lived with my first serious girlfriend after leaving the RAF. One day we decided to pack our bags and jet off on holiday together to sunnier skies. A month later I saw a deal on TV teletext service *(the early prehistoric version of Google)*. We saw ourselves land in Corfu and were to begin a week-long holiday which was something completely new to me and I relished the prospect. I'd been all over the world and covered most aspects of personal recreation, but it was with my career parents, 'Mummy and Daddy' Air Force.

To say it didn't begin *'quite'* as we planned was an understatement! As we landed and waited for our luggage we were informed by a holiday representative that the local baggage handlers had *'all of a sudden'* voted in the last hour to go on strike, and our bags would be brought to us by a relief crew who were being sourced as we spoke. Fantastic, deep joy - It was about 31° outside. But within the baggage halls it must have been more around 40° plus and the air more carbon dioxide than oxygen.

Eventually the bags found their merry way to our coach and after about four hours of sweating and cursing we soon saw the sights of down town Corfu town as we took the low road along the base of the mountain that looked across to the tips and peaks of the Albanian mountain range. It was a beautiful and majestic sight to behold.

We were systematically ejected from our coach with our luggage and told to walk just further down and we would see where we were staying. It all seemed to be very 'hurried' if you want my take on it.

I soon discovered exactly why the coach driver was reluctant to drop us off in front of the building and preferred to park a hundred metres away.

As the coach pulled off, if I didn't know any better I'd say that those on the back seat were looking back at us with hands over their mouths in an attempt to mask their hysterical laughter. I was tired, hot but yes I was right, people were in hysterics, looking at what was supposed to be our digs for a week.

They really WERE laughing. What an absolute dung pile! As we took our luggage up the rickety wooden staircase past the table of local mafia playing poker in what I think might have started out as a local café below, we got to the top and a hand pushed the creaking door open to reveal a single room.

There was no furniture apart from a single bed and an old wooden wardrobe which, I would think *had* at some point in its life stored a dead body or two judging by the smell.

Oh boy! Liz went into complete meltdown. I remember it with extreme clarity. I'm not going to make light of it or try and present it in a couched framework of cynicism or grey humour.

She was a cross between upset and livid with a hint of depression. I was surprisingly calm. I'm not sure why to be honest? I think looking back I had probably used up most of my anger credits at the airport when one of the local airport workers said it was not his problem, but ours.

He had baggage written on his white coloured overalls and was sunbathing outside the main hall with his friend as they pointed and sniggered. He decided it was hilarious but we didn't. So here we were. Stuck in what had all the splendour of a chicken shack (that would actually have smelled better to be honest) and two large suitcases with two very hot and tired hacked off tourists.

We'd been had! Sorry, *I* had been had. Liz had nothing to do with it and just trusted my judgement. It would appear I had let her down. Fantastically bad if that's an acceptable adjective? Wherever you are now Liz, I apologise profoundly.

I switched to military mode in a heartbeat and decided on an action plan. We needed to extract ourselves from this place with immediate effect and not cause any raised eyebrows.. I told Liz to leave the building as calmly as possible the way we came in. Then turn left outside the door and head (calmly) towards the telephone box next to the cigarette kiosk in the square. It must have been about two hundred meters away. I would grab our two cases and make my exit out of the back door.

We both reached the telephone box chain smoking wondering what to do next. Liz suggested we call our travel agent in Canterbury. She picked up the phone and over three or four calls were re-directed to another agent who to me appeared to be wasting time and passing the buck.

Liz was becoming more frustrated and angry and at one point almost collapsed in the booth trying her best to negotiate at least a return flight home. Yes, it had now got to the point where we were prepared to actually cut our losses and run. I will admit I was very distressed, not angry. I was at a height of concern which I had never experienced before in my life. I really loved and cared for my girlfriend. I'd never seen any woman get this upset and it was beginning to eat away at my resolve. I felt numb with sadness, void of energy and purpose. I never ever want to experience that feeling again. It was at this point that I found myself praying.

Yep. The cards had been dealt and life looked desperate so what else was there to do.

I remember exactly what I said too.

"Okay. So here I am, stuck and it's crap. I will take full responsibility for it. I screwed up guys. I really screwed up bad. But here's the thing. Liz doesn't deserve this. She really doesn't and I'm asking now for your Divine help. Please. I need your help to get us out of this, not for me, but for her. I love her and watching her in this state is killing me. Please help her. Please?"

Liz put the phone down relatively calmly and walked slowly out of the booth into my arms. She had just had enough and sought comfort. I hadn't told her about my pleading with the Universe for help. She just said the agents would ring back in half an hour (again) and we were to stay near the phones for further advice.

So, there we sat. On a wall smoking and wondering just how we could possibly get out of this mess. After nearly an hour we had both agreed we would call friends and family and see if they could help out by transferring cash to allow us to get to the airport and fly back after roughing it on the beach for the night. We were shattered, emotionally drained and just completely void of interest in anything, other than we were thirsty and desperately needed water.

But that was all about to change.

I'm never going to forget what happened next. We were draped over a wall trying to stay awake when a Mercedes car pulled up about fifty feet from us.

"Hey? You English from Canterbury?

I looked at Liz. She looked at me. We both looked at the driver and with a slightly cautious response I answered "Yes".

"You both are coming with me - yes? I take you to your new hotel?" We both again had to double check we weren't imagining it but again I took the lead and agreed after a couple of security questions to go with him. Where was this hotel? Where would he be taking us?

Who has instructed him to take us? If the door locks go down, get ready...

As we stood by his car door, I remember thinking that outwardly, this guy did seem pretty genuine. He came across a very nice friendly family man who probably couldn't fathom why these two English tourists would have such a problem accepting a ride in his *(rather swish it must be said)* taxi. And so, we got in.

More questions were fired at this poor guy and he explained he just got a call to collect two people at the phones with our surnames and take them to his best friend's hotel which was five miles further down the coast. I asked no more questions but as we arrived it got even more confusing.

I turned to Liz as the nice man took our luggage from the boot whistling as he did all the way to the entrance.

"Hang on! Hang on! We can't afford this? It's a prince's palace! We better check all the small print because this might seem good, however it could bite us in the ass?"

As I'd finished putting my two pence worth in, a man sauntered down to the gates and just said:

"My friends, my friends - welcome, welcome, welcome! I formerly welcome you to my hotel. Yes, and before you ask many questions, let me explain to you answers. You have been given a week stay here with me and I have your room all ready. You do not need to pay, no. Pay from England already yes? I have been told to take good care of you. I know England as I went to Oxford many times and have friends there. I am very happy that you stay with us here. Please, let me take you to the bar first for a drink. You must be quite thirsty?"

The barman then thrusts two of the best Singapore Slings I have ever tasted into our hands. I felt I had died and gone to heaven. We were then escorted to our rooms where our luggage had already been positioned by the door. Well, what a sight! I had never to this day seen such a smart, exquisite apartment. It was jaw dropping. I don't think Liz said a great deal. She was still in shock repeating the question under her breath.

"So we don't pay? This is all for us? It's sorted? We're safe and sound? Our holiday is well and truly back on with a bang?"

It was, very much so. That holiday was simply magnificent. We had beautiful days on the beach and hired a motorcycle to go sightseeing the island together. I will always look back on that moment in my life as the point where a clear demonstration of assistance was given to me. It was given to us, and here's why I think it happened. I asked for help. But I didn't ask for help for *myself*. I pleaded for help for Liz. That's the difference.

The Universe was watching. The Universe was listening. I asked the Universe for emergency assistance. The Universe obliged and I am still and always will, be eternally grateful for that day.

Above all else without a definitive, it is my belief that Angels came to our rescue.

That 'dung heap' we found ourselves in initially actually delivered us to better things. Hindsight saw us having to 'go through the mill' first and then just as it looked like we were done, a beautiful stunning watering hole appeared in the desert haze and it was no mirage, it was most certainly real.

There were two lessons to be learned here:

- Firstly, like a seed, sometimes you have to be suffocated and buried in horse manure five feet under in total darkness, only to then rise up breaking free into the pure air to flower and bathe in the serenity of the light.

- Secondly, learn to ask for help. It's on tap. It's there and what's more it can assist. You are not judged by spirits and angels. They love you and want to advise and help on a daily basis.

THE SPIRITUAL VEIL

There are a great many accounts of people waking up in the middle of the night to see *Aunty Doreen* standing at the end of their bed. Also accounts describing sightings of people that have long since passed, sitting at their favourite table spot in a restaurant or in their armchair at home. I have to state I would not try to discredit these accounts, there has to be a cross section of maybe three completely different types of encounter:

- ♥ The first one where *Aunty Doreen* was seen standing at the base of the bed, belongs to the 'Spirit Check-ins'. Normally a one-stop-shop of a glimpse of a visitor. For reasons that we shall never really understand, our relatives come and visit us for all manner of private reasons. It might be because their children (even in their fifties or sixties) are unwell or experiencing a very traumatic period in their lives. It could be their anniversary, or quite literally anything. They cross the one-way street which is known as the Spiritual Veil where they can manifest into our time and space, but we cannot theirs.

- ♥ This second category should ring a few bells with either yourself or your parents or, you as parents. Small children of an age up to about three are new to this realm and time space. They are pure of heart and consciousness and often still interact with where they travelled from. The next time you witness a baby pointing and speaking in their own way to someone but there doesn't appear to be anyone there, don't dismiss it. They are more than likely playing with your parents who have passed or family in spirit. The sadness that surrounds grandparents when they never live long enough to hold their grandchildren in their arms can be exchanged for 'visitation rights' from spirit. This time however, it is the baby being able to see *them* rather than *'them'* being in our time-space. Just as the very frail and old have the same ability at the end of their lives to see the spirit world. *'Where do you think imaginary friends came from, and also those seen talking to invisible people on their death-beds?'*

♥ The third category of accounts which describe apparitions and ghosts are just that. 'Ghosts'. There is a distinct difference between this and the previous two categories. A Spirit is the manifestation of itself as a former human being, familiar to those whom they now appear. Not always as they were in age, but commonly as they would be recognised. It is widely believed that when we pass, we begin to revert in Earth-age and appearance to a *'time period during our last experience'* where we were vibrant, healthy and youthful. If your grandad appeared to you as a twenty-five-year old you'd have no idea who it was, and so to ensure you know exactly who it is, they tend to appear at whatever age they want.

My personal definition of a ghost is the sighting of a recording in the ether. I find this concept fascinating. The fact that as beings of energy, we are capable of leaving a full imprint in this 'time-space' for anyone else to tune in and see a section of our existence within it is truly amazing.

I have been the subject of a ghost story which, I still *to this day* lose a little sleep over, especially seeing how I'm still here!

I visited my good friends Richard and Anne-Marie (Murray) at their home in Norfolk. Richie and Murray were *(and still are)* like extended family to me from my days in the military. I was sitting in their living room and Murray pipes up with one of those panicky explanations that you have, when you suddenly remember something.

"Oh. Hogi!" said Richard. "Yes" I replied.

"Oh wait a minute. Richard..." Murray interrupted. *"Do you remember what happened when we went to JHQ in Germany?"*

Like a lightning bolt had hit Richie he shouts.

"Ah. Yes! Yes! We saw you Hogi. Yes, that's right. Well, Murray did. I remember now."

I'm now scratching my head carrying out some quick-fire calculations in my head and the figures aren't adding up.

"You saw me - in JHQ - in Germany?"

"Yes." replied Murray. *"You were standing outside the NAAFI shop where they sell all the duty free hi-fi and all that stuff."*

"When was this?" I asked.

"Oh, it was when we were out there some time back. I can't remember exactly." She replied.

I'm now completely bemused.

"But, if it was when you were posted out there, then I had already left the RAF. I had left RAF Germany long in my wake. Some eight years in my wake in fact."

"I know. But I definitely saw you. I know it was you because you smiled at me. I will never forget that. It really shook me up. I thought, Oh my word! There's Hogi! And you smiled. Same flat top haircut. Same saunter. Then, just as you appeared... You vanished. It was the most bizarre thing. It shocked me, and I became quite emotional."

"She's not lying to you mate. Ann-Marie definitely saw you. It was you all right."

I am now sitting on their sofa with a coffee trying to get my head around what I've just *heard*.

"So, let me sum up and try and get this straight. You saw me in a place that I was last physically in over eight years prior to you being there. I could not have been there at that moment, because I know I

never went back to JHQ and to this day still haven't. So, just how is that possible?"

Murray then suggests a possible explanation:

"Well, it's said that sometimes, humans can leave an imprint. We can leave a sort of recording of ourselves and only those close to you can tune into it. You can normally leave a recording of your life at a moment of extreme emotional stress."

"Well, that all fits sure enough but why the NAAFI at JHQ?" I asked.

"Were you going through a traumatic period of your life then Hogi?"

I sat there for a few moments and then felt like a train just ran over my soul.

"You remember something significant then?" Murray asks.

"Yes, it just smacked me in the face. Gulf War. JHQ was a place that I used to go quite a lot with Pete, Keith, Rab, Al and a few other guys. Lee had been posted back to the UK on his fitter's course, so he wouldn't have been there. I think it was coming up to Christmas 1990 and we were informed that all leave was cancelled due to TTW (Transition to War).

I remember us all wandering around like lost sheep, and JHQ seemed to be a good place to go to bring back some sort of normality to the insane suggestion that we now faced. Yes. I do remember going there and buying a CD, Propaganda 1234. Blimey. The things you recall eh?"

Murray looked across at me with a sad face.

"So that was the last place you were emotionally tied to before flying out to war?"

"Yep, indeed, it was."

"Well Hogi, all I know is I saw you very briefly. I saw you in the clothes that you would a year or so later be wearing when we first met at Henlow upon your posting back to the UK. It was you and nobody will tell me otherwise."

I looked at Richie and he said nothing, just smiled and raised his eyebrows.

This is not something you generally hear every day, is it? But how thought provoking was that do you think? It isn't invented or fabricated. It's the truth. As I type this, I know that one person will know it's the truth and possibly the answer to this for certain because she's now back home in spirit. Anne-Marie (Murray) lost her battle with breast cancer whilst I was living with my first wife. I had no idea of this until a friend had the painful job of telling me. To say it upset me doesn't even begin to scratch the surface. To this day my heart has never fully repaired from the scars of the day I found out.

"I miss you Murray. I love you so much. I'm sorry I wasn't there my darling."

Finding out my best friend in the whole world had died and I was nowhere to be seen has haunted me to this day. I was so consumed and bitter, it was the nail that finally told me my life wasn't right. Something about this whole scenario was painfully wrong and only I could do something about it.

That coupled with what my ex-wife did in a bid to keep me from my daughter more than likely pushed my heart over the edge and that led me to CCU, but here's the thing. I remember distinctly, without any mistake, looking up to the heavens after leaving my ex-wife and saying to the Universe, *"Come on. Is this going to be how my life goes? Why can't you find me someone like Anne-Marie?"*

One week later I met Tina. I cannot put into words just how awesome this woman is, but let's just say my prayers were answered. And I still wonder to this day whether Murray was looking down and guiding me along a path where Tina and I were destined to meet.

I am eternally grateful for her being in my life and helping to shape who I really am.

Was that invisible assistance? Oh, I'd say so, without a shadow of doubt! Thank you, Murray.

CHAPTER TWELVE

Opening Doors

"One of the greatest gifts in life is being able to rest your head on your pillow at night with piece of mind and piece of heart."

After what seemed a long battle, my nine-year first marriage was ending. It was a terrifying feeling. I thought at one point I might have Bi-polar. I would go from a calm emotional, rational mental state of mind to feelings of suicide in a flash. I knew I had to separate myself from that place of dark energy and sadness but there was just one thing holding me back - my one-year old daughter.

Those last weeks were a mixture of coming home, saying very little and attending to Ellie-Mae, then in the morning off to work for weeks at a time staying away in Northern Ireland which in retrospect was actually good for both of us.

Fast forward a year and I met my present wife Tina. To be quite honest, I wasn't really looking for another relationship; I was exhausted and just wanted a friend. A chance encounter at a hotel in Scotland saw us meet when a fire alarm went off and we all filed outside. That's where I just said "hello," and the next thing I knew, everyone had gone in and we were left standing there enjoying each other's company.

Over a period of time we became very good friends and that escalated into best friends. We were totally inseparable. On an hourly basis I kept myself in check knowing I should be careful. I felt like the equivalent of a zoo lion that's been released into the wild after nine years in a cage.

I was trying to keep my emotions and words in check. However, deep down, I knew I had found the woman for me. It did all seem far too good to be true. Eventually the situation got a lot better and kept getting better.

I left home and moved into Tina's house, but dark clouds were never far away, and one day a situation arose where my previous conditioning and state of mind saw me lose control, quite badly. Initially my ex-wife and I were pretty good together. Yes, we had potential. But, over time, we both in equal measure had our issues and they were quite a potent mix when challenged.

My ex-wife was a great Mum; I could never take that away from her. Despite our differences and divorce, I knew without a shadow of doubt that my daughter was going to be just fine. I may not have got it right for me, but I sure got it right for my little girl. But when I had moved on I received a letter from my ex-wife's solicitors and to say it made me angry is not even scratching the surface. Not even close.

It was some time during late 2011 and I was pacing up and down our kitchen, absolutely livid. I never intended abandoning my little girl. No chance. I wanted my entitled rights to see her and I was going to pay my child support. But that wasn't going to be that straight forward.

Now then, that 'S' word - Stress. I don't think I need to tell anyone that cigarettes are bad for you. Alcohol in constant supply isn't exactly brilliant (though at the time it may feel like it!) Couple all three with excessive carbohydrate intake and it's not looking good. Stress though, is a killer.

If you're middle aged and you have any weakness in your heart area, stress will find you and it will very quickly let you know it's found you. After pacing up and down the kitchen with Tina and her friend Emma trying their best to calm me down, I said I was going to the gym for a work-out.

Off I went, and the punch bag got it bad. I think I cycled about ten miles at electric pace and then hit the steam room. When I got home I did actually feel better. *(So, I thought)*. But the situation wasn't ever far from the surface. My every waking thought saw danger around the corner and it wouldn't take much to trip the switch. So, off to bed we went, and it was lights out. It had been a very stressful day. I woke up at 1:20am a little confused and not entirely sure why. Something didn't feel right. I felt very strange. Tina stirred and immediately asked me if I was ok. I explained the latter and she calmly leaned across and put her left ear to my chest.

"I think it's best if you get dressed darling. I'll do the same and we'll just pop to the hospital."

I was in borderline panic mode, confused and very worried but I knew that something was wrong with my heart and worrying wasn't making the situation better.

I was worried that worrying would make things worse so I tried to stop, but it just wasn't happening! I did have some thoughts on this brand-new experience though.

"Right, so.... this is how I go? This is how I die? Is it going to hurt much? Can't we just get it over with and not draw it out then? Oh, but wait, what about Tina? We've only just met? Great! I find real happiness and boom! I'm done, fantastic. "Cheers, thanks for that."

We got to the hospital with Tina's calm and measured approach and eventually I ended up in CCU all plugged in looking like I was radio controlled. After a whole day lying on the bed, and with no let up my heart was still racing away at over 200bpm. I was running what I think was my third marathon, but hadn't actually moved a muscle. The nurses were angels, fantastic people.

"Right Mr Hogan, you've been on Potassium and another drip medication now for a few hours, if nothing changes in the next hour, we'll place you on the list for Defibrillation- okay?"

'De' what - holy meatballs - really?

I began to panic slightly. Being ex-Mountain Rescue Team in the Forces I knew exactly what that meant and had seen it for real. It's where they place electrode paddles across your chest and after 120-200 Joules of 'whap' they 'zap' you. This is normally to restart the heart after it stops. What if this stopped it for good? I was now in a kind of transition curve. I remember the strange acceptance of it all, like I had been told by some invisible energy. *"Just stop being a big baby and just get on with it."*

Opposite my bed there was an elderly gentleman who was waiting to be taken to theatre for what I assumed was an operation on his heart. A Priest walked in carrying a Bible and initially walked towards my bed. I knew he would turn left, and he did. With a quick swoosh of the curtains he went about his business and prayed with the lovely man. It really didn't help the situation, a reminder of the balance between here and... well, who knows? Back then I still wasn't really sure what happens or where we go. It wasn't something I had thought about – Death!

Oh, my life I don't know? What if there's nothing? What if I go to hell! I'm going to fry.

What if there really is - you know...

Then the oddest thing happened which I will never forget. Tina saw me looking at the Priest and knew that coupled with the threat of shocking and zapping me out of my condition, I wasn't in a good place. She could see that I was now becoming quite emotional and my eyes were watering. She just leaned across the bed and slowly kissed me on the lips whispering, "I love you Mr H."

Hang on? What is...? I feel very odd again what's happening?

Oh, oh my. Oh, this feels good.

A nurse then swiftly glides across from around the monitoring station supporting a grin the size of a Cheshire Cat.

"So, Mr Hogan, how do we feel now? Better?"

I felt ecstatic. It was a combination of total joy, laughter, exhilaration all at once. My heart suddenly reset all on its own, just as Tina kissed me.

"Hang on a minute!" Tina looked at me and then at the nurse who was smiling.

"Isn't it supposed to be the other way around? You're supposed to make my heart flutter?"

And so, after a further evaluation overnight, I went home the next day and was off work for four weeks rest.

That's where events took an interesting turn.

THE WOMAN IN THE NIGHT

One night after a week or so, I was lying in bed next to Tina who was well away with the fairies.

I recall feeling totally relaxed, and my state of mind was a little anxious, but I was in a good place. I'd had far too much sleep lately that perhaps it was payback. My body just wasn't tired, so I just lay there motionless listening to Tina muttering. She seemed to be talking and murmuring but when asking her in the morning she had no recollection of it!

I turned onto my left side and tried to sleep yet again. I thought that if I carried out some slow controlled deep breathing exercises it might help. So, I did just that. I do remember being slightly dozy, that feeling of nearly being asleep but not quite. I remember my eyes trying to open but I was resisting, trying to keep the momentum of the warm and relaxed feeling. Then 'a woman' appeared, right in front of my face.

She was not staring down at me as I was lying on my left side looking at the wall. She was sitting or kneeling with her upper body facing me as if she was at my hospital bed visiting.

She was just 'there,' looking directly at me.

Hang on? I thought. It's totally dark? How come I can see you? I closed my eyes again and she disappeared from view. Then, when I opened them, there she was! She wasn't one of the 'visions' I'd read about from the third eye. I was seeing her in real time. I can't really use words to describe her or my feelings toward her. But I loved her instantly and completely. I almost felt her absorbing my consciousness and melding into my actual 'being'.

She didn't speak with her mouth. I sort of had a 'knowing,' as if she had downloaded a thought into my mind.

"You're going to be okay Noel."

Then she very slowly smiled, a slight comforting smile and she was gone. That's all I got. But this woman was incredibly beautiful. I feel shivers and goose bumps still thinking about her. It was so hard to explain. If you take sexual love and combine that with parental love you feel toward your parents or how you would feel toward your child, then the love you feel toward your pet when it's not well, you just scratch the surface of what it was I felt that night when that lady appeared to me.

It was a very special moment which I will never forget. But it left me asking a great deal of questions. I saw a doorway that I'd not seen before, and I was totally intrigued. My thirst for knowledge was insatiable. Maybe there is a life after this? Maybe there is this Spirit World where we all go?

Maybe, just maybe, she answered my question when I was in hospital. Is there a Spirit World? Well I'm sure going to try and find out! As you can imagine, when something happens to you in life that is a complete smack in the face your path will change. You will without consciously knowing it, change course on another coordinate and the journey takes on another objective.

I began to read books about the Spirit World. Upon reading book after book, a pattern began to form. Each book didn't so much repeat the same scenarios and facts; moreover it stressed the same message again and again. Using a cliché, the covers were different but the stories all remained the same.

LOVE! This is what I was being told time and time and time again. It's all about love, nothing else. Love is the goal here on Earth - to love.

So, a roller coaster ride of text intake would consume me for a few years and it soon became a passion. Again though, I had another thing happen to me consecutively for three nights which like the vision of the lady, took me aback and set me off again on a quest for answers.

After a meditation exercise one evening I went to bed and thought little more. Then, I began to wake up after only what seemed ten minutes. It was if some goon with his car headlights on full beam had driven up to our bedroom window, with the light increasing its power until it was like looking directly into the midday summer sun.

Given that our bedroom was on the first floor this seemed like quite a challenge. Also, the curtains were drawn and blackout roller blinds pulled down to block out the street lights. So, if it wasn't a car? What was it?

I think it's very important at this juncture to state for the record that despite what you might think, I'm not the sort of person to jump to a conclusion that fits what I would wish it to be. I'm actually quite flexible and open minded about strange happenings.

If a bright light appears that's all encompassing and blinding, a first thought might be "It's a 'supernatural encounter' with something not of this world," and maybe that might be correct. There is always a logical explanation for everything, if it was a supernatural encounter then that's fine. But it may well have been self-induced or, something wrong with a link between my mind and my vision. There's just one element in all of this however that seals the deal for me. It isn't always something which we give our attention to when we witness strange phenomena or something which we cannot fully explain, which is the main message of this whole book.

I would agree with anyone that when that 'lady' appeared by my bedside, being in a particular state of relaxation things *can* happen, it is a well-known and documented fact that when the human body is so relaxed you *can* hallucinate. It's a fact and I agree with the science of it. However, and it's a big however. I saw with my eyes, but as we know, eyes are not only viewers.

Eyes are also projectors. When my vision was woken with this strange powerful yellow glow, there was something else that came with it, a feeling, an emotion, all encompassing – LOVE. Just like the lady who appeared before me at my bed side, not only did I see her, but I *felt* her love and it wasn't an affectionate love or like a puppy love. Oh no. This was a fifty-metre-high 'tsunami' of the purest love heading toward a beach of doubt. It hit me like I'd been through a spiritual car wash with extra suds. That light woke me up and dropped me in a vat of warm chocolate. I felt so at ease with it and devoured by its presence that I just didn't want it to end. It's not only what I see, but what I *feel* that guides me to what I believe.

I have no idea to this day why, or where or for what reason, but it was quite beautiful. If the same has happened to you, then be sure to let me know.

A SPIRITUAL PHENOMENON

The third and final demonstration of Spiritual Phenomena arrived some two years later when again, I went to sleep and this time it had been a couple of hours and then it happened. But I will give you a little background on what led up to this first.

I had been visiting a very good family friend of Tina for a day at our local hospital, the same one which I was in with a dodgy ticker. He told me on several occasions that we were very similar. He never really engaged with me much because he didn't really know me that well, but he knew Tina very well and adored her. Feeling like a 'Spiritual Jedi', I realised the significance of reading peoples' energy upon initial contact. I do this unconsciously now and will always trust it. He was a beautiful kind loving man. His energy had this nailed and he was such a cheeky chap. The nurses were never going to forget him, but there was a serious problem. We knew it and he did too but, like any of us tried to brush it aside and pretend that it was all just a bad dream.

Whilst in the ward I asked his stepdaughter if I could talk with him on my level and she said yes. It was at this point she made her exit, gave her father a hug and told him that she would pop in tomorrow. I'm not shy of confronting awkward questions. It doesn't matter whether it is my own father or a stranger. I will go in direct and not beat around the bush, so I asked him the following:

"Listen, you know that things aren't good - yes? You know there's a problem and you're anxious because they're taking a biopsy and you'll get the results in a couple of days, so, I need to ask you a very important question. Are you okay with me asking you?"

He nodded and said it was fine.

"All of us want nothing more than a good result and for you to get the 'all-clear'. We want you to go home to your family and for them to sort out your fencing and access requirements. But here's the thing, I

need to ask you and it isn't pretty. If the result comes back and the news isn't what you'd hoped for, and your time is handed to you on a calendar, are you prepared to face this?"

His response was surprisingly measured at first. He explained that death wasn't the issue. He wasn't frightened of death which was reassuring to hear. However, in seconds he welled up and became extremely upset explaining:

"I'm scared of the pain Noel. I don't want to spend months and months in pain. I don't want it to happen like it did to my brother."

He was totally inconsolable. I felt I'd made things worse not better and now he would remember me for all the wrong reasons. Fantastic! Then, without warning I heard something come out of my mouth which to be brutally honest shocked me... Normally, before I speak, the words will have been supervised and undergone 'Hogan Quality Control' prior to being shipped out. Not this time though. They came right out, and nothing was going to stop them.

"Listen to me. Listen. You are NOT going to suffer. I can tell you right now. Your brother is going to make sure of it. They'll be no suffering. No pain. He's going to come and see you and ask you if you are ready to leave for 'home'.

No pain okay? You're going to be just fine. Just fine"

In a way, the conversation kind of 'suggested' what the biopsy was going to say. It felt a little arrogant saying what I did. But as I explained to Tina, there was just no way to stop it coming out. I was just as surprised as everyone else. It did seem like I was being 'channelled'.

The next couple of days went by, and upon arriving home after a day at work I looked at Tina standing in the kitchen with her mobile phone in her hand. She looked up with no particular fixed expression, so I knew it was a moment of clarity coming. I just didn't know what kind of clarity.

"I've had a text," she said.

Then I definitely knew what was coming.

"He passed away this morning - peacefully."

Tears followed. Both of us hugged and we agreed that it was a kind of relief; both for him and his family. I recall feeling pleased for him. He got what he so wanted, a pain-free final chapter. "I told you so!" I thought with a cheeky smile on my face. What came to me that night though was a complete surprise!

Again, I was fast asleep, and I was being woken but without my physical eyes being open, consciously not sub-consciously. I need to stress to you that it is quite difficult to actually describe what happened to me, but I can only use the adjectives available within the context of our spoken word.

I'd had a normal day. I don't drink, or smoke and drugs are definitely off limits. As I became 'aware' of something strange happening I felt compelled to open my eyes. As I did so there was just the blackness of night – nothing! I closed my eyes tightly shut - sure enough something was closing into view, a ball of light. This ball was fascinating, it was a beautiful colour, a mesh of blue and purple but as if there were segments of its skin that allowed you to see inside.

The inside was glowing with a bright yellow/white light. I can't tell you if it was five inches in diameter or the size of the sun. I had no idea of size, it was quite odd. I have told this to Mediums and other energy healers and explained that it was very similar to those infrared live images of our sun taken by NASA. Once into view, a sound accompanied it. This sound did seem quite familiar. I'd love to tell you that it was the magnified vibration of fairies stroking the wings of celestial heavenly butterflies on a fluffy cotton cloud, but no. Strangely, it sounded like trains slowly manoeuvring across points in a large station.

Seriously, it was just that, a metal on metal sound. Now you'd think wouldn't you that this hasn't got the makings of a very pleasant experience? But I can tell you, just like the other unexplainable encounters, this one too had a feeling associated with it. An unmistakable *feeling* - LOVE! It's that pesky 'Love' again!

Somehow, I thought I knew who it was. I will never claim to know for definite, but I do have my suspicions. I think you might too. I think he came to say 'thanks'. I hope so, it would mean a great deal to me. Ironically though, I never actually said those words of comfort to him the last time I saw him.

It was another soul in Spirit using me as the 'messenger'. Something I was going to have to get used to...

It's all about living your true-life purpose in accordance with the Universal Life Force.

CHAPTER THIRTEEN

Meditation

"Meditation is the discovery that the point of life is always arrived at in the immediate moment."

Alan Watts

Ah! That meditation thing, I just knew he'd bring it up. I've been waiting for this bit:

- I've tried it a hundred times.
- What the heck does it do when you CAN do it?
- How do I know that I *am* doing it?
- Do I have to sit crossed legged in the lotus position and chant mantras?
- What does meditation mean?
- What does it do?

I elected to ask these questions on your behalf because it's just so obvious a set of questions to ask by anyone and everyone who's ever considered meditation. I'm fascinated by it as I see it as a key to a much more intense personal experience and link to the spirit self.

Synonyms of the word are as follows:

- contemplation
- thought
- thinking
- musing
- pondering
- consideration
- reflection
- prayer/deliberation
- study
- rumination
- cogitation
- brooding
- mulling over

Without presenting the subject in an over-scientific way, what you need to know about meditation is that it means to empty the mind, 'creating space for rent'. Now if you've had a clear out and you've made space, who is going to want to use it if it isn't you? Have a think... I'll give you a little clue.

Our friend in Alcatraz had all the time in the world to think and you can bet that after he had accepted his fate, he really had very little to occupy his mind. Nothing to worry or clutter up his thought process. So, do you think a higher authority came to rent that space to add value to his own thinking and remind him of what he really was?

Another example of meditation is when 'mediums' clear their mind and place their human consciousness in a set frequency enabling space for 'visitors.' But they too will always state that you don't really need a medium to forge this connection. You have the capacity to link with spirits. My good friend and 'Spirit Artist' *Sandy Ingham* places herself into an altered state to be able to receive guided physical instruction by the hand of her guide. She then draws with her hands, but Meditation can also be singing.

When you're singing it's very difficult to worry or focus on anything other than your song. Meditation can also be carried out by colouring in a book of pictures. In fact, this has actually been around for thousands of years but received a kind of re-birth recently.

I've meditated very often simply by using ambient, emotionally lifting music on my phone. It's pretty awesome stuff I can tell you. The typical stereotypical monk or zen-master sitting in the lotus position isn't all about meditation. It is merely a single example of yoga and relaxation which leads to a personal experience which in most cases is a meditation of one form or another.

Types of Meditation

Scientists usually classify meditation based on the way they focus attention into two categories:

- Focused Attention
- Open Monitoring

Focused Attention Meditation

This is focusing the attention on a single object during the whole meditation session. This object may be the breath, a mantra, visualization, part of the Body, external object, etc. As the practitioner advances, his ability to keep the flow of attention in the chosen object gets stronger, and distractions become less common and short-lived. Both the depth and steadiness of his attention are developed.

Examples of these are:

- Samantha Mediation - A Buddhist Meditation
- Some forms of Zazen
- Loving Kindness Meditation
- Chakra Meditation
- Kundalini Meditation
- Sound Meditation
- Mantra Meditation
- Pranayama
- Some forms of Qigong and many others

Open Monitoring Meditation

Instead of focusing the attention on any one object, we keep it open, monitoring all aspects of our experience, without judgment or attachment.

All perceptions, be them internal (thoughts, feelings, memory, etc.) or external (sound, smell, etc.), are recognized and seen for what they are. It is the process of non-reactive monitoring of the content of experience from moment to moment, without going into them.

Examples are:

- Mindfulness Meditation
- Vipassana
- As well as some types of Taoist Meditation

Effortless Presence

It's the state where the attention is not focused on anything in particular, but reposes on itself – quiet, empty, steady, and introverted. We can also call it "Choice-less Awareness" or "Pure Being". Most of the meditation quotes you find speak of this state. This is actually the true purpose behind all kinds of meditation, and not a meditation type in itself. All traditional techniques of meditation recognize that the object of focus, and even the process of monitoring, is just a *means* to train the mind, so that effortless inner silence and deeper states of consciousness can be discovered. Eventually both the object of focus and the process itself is left behind, and there is only left the true self of the practitioner, as "pure presence."

THE PINEAL GLAND

There's one area I mentioned previously when connected to *'lack of thinking'* or meditation, can open up the potential for you to be a walking, breathing, talking 'super-human', and believe me, I'm not over playing it either, please trust me on this. If you go to your browser tool and type in the following:

"What do spiritual people who meditate use their pineal (third eye) gland for?" This is what you should expect to find:

"The pineal gland, a pine-cone shaped gland of the endocrine system, is a highly essential part of the brain necessary to our survival. It is often associated with the third eye or the Ajna chakra, which when activated, leads one to higher realms of consciousness. The third eye gives us perception of the Universe around us through the five senses."

Through our five senses we have self-awareness and intelligence: sentience.

As a chakra, the third eye, the *pineal gland* represents the point at which the body receives energy from the Universe, the main access point between the astral body and the physical body. Its function in the brain is essential to our very consciousness.

Without awareness of the Universe, you have no point of reference at which you have self-awareness and without self-awareness, you have neither consciousness nor logical thought. We use our perception, our consciousness and our senses to gain awareness of energy in our world via information around us. Without the pineal gland there would be no senses, meaning we would have no way to locate food, our mates, safety, warmth, and the many necessities of everyday life.

CHAPTER FOURTEEN

The Near Death Experience

"There was a small light and I really wanted to move toward it, but I didn't know why."

Nothing I am about to say would raise an eyebrow in the communities I roam about with on my Facebook networks and close friends so let us examine the term then. What does it truly mean and who invented it?

Near-death experience (NDE) was given its name by Doctor Raymond Moody and is a personal experience associated with death or impending death, encompassing multiple possible sensations including detachment from the body, feelings of levitation, total serenity, security, warmth, the experience of absolute dissolution, and the presence of a light. Explanatory models for the NDE can be divided into several broad categories. (Research from neuroscience considers the NDE to be a hallucinatory state caused by various physiological and psychological factors).

I have elected to state in that last sentence that there are a percentage of professional scientists who regard NDE states to be nothing more than residual electrical energy and a hallucinatory effect brought about by the death and subsequent shut down of the brain. I respect all peoples' opinions and think that it is important to hear both arguments on this hot topic. I wish to state however, for the record, that I am a true believer in the concept of the NDE. I have absolutely no doubt whatsoever that we are eternal beings and we inhabit this body to experience a lower vibrational existence; to love, to hate, to fear, to judge, to laugh and cry.

LORNA'S STORY

I first heard about NDEs when we were finishing up after a long and tiring day on the mountain training.

"I died once. I did. I died after being hit by a car when I was seven. I saw my body and all of the ambulance medics trying to get me back. I was hovering around near the chimney of my dad's house where I ran out onto the road and then I just started moving what seemed like upwards, but I wasn't sure.

There was a small light and I really wanted to move toward it, but I didn't know why. It was fast though. Like speed of light fast. I then thought I was back, but I wasn't.

It just looked like earth but then when I looked properly it was much more beautiful and there was a strange feeling of joy too. The flowers were colours I'd never seen and then next to them was our dog Betty. She died a year ago and my Mum was very sad. She licked my face. There was air, but it had like, music to it. I can't explain it.

I saw my Mum's two sisters and my grandad. They came across and hugged me and there were loads of other people. Some I recognised and some I didn't but, I kind of felt like I should?

I asked if I could stay but my grandad had a friend with him and he sort of glowed like on the porridge advert. He was a beautiful colour and I felt so safe and warm near him. I couldn't see his face as it was just light. He said if I saw his face I would have to stay. He said I cannot stay as it wasn't my time. I must go back to my earthly body because I have not completed my mission.

Then all of a sudden I woke up and I was in hospital and my mum was crying with her head on my shoulder and I asked her why and she jumped up all hysterical and started screaming and laughing calling my dad and brother to come over from the nurses' station quickly."

I remember that conversation quite well. I wasn't so much intrigued, more, gobsmacked.

"So, you just got hit by a car? And you were killed? I get that bit. That's fine. Well, it isn't fine, but it is from an understanding viewpoint. You know what I'm trying to say... Then, you travelled to heaven?"

"If you want to call it that - I have no issue, but I would call it home."

"Okay, let's call it home or Spirit World then. So, you go home and then come back?"

"Yes."

"What - just like that?"

"Yes - just like that."

"How long were you dead for, do you mind me asking?"

"No that's fine, not at all. It was twenty-nine years ago but I still have all the clinical details right here." (She reached for newspaper clippings from the local Herald).

"I was clinically dead for 43 minutes."

"But I thought science has proven that the brain is dead through oxygen starvation in about four minutes?

"Yes quite possibly."

"So, how come you're still fine then?"

"Let me ask you a question Noel."

"Fire away...."

"Who do you think created the world - the stars, the whole known Universe and the intricacies of the tiniest living organisms known to science?"

"That's easy, God, or the Source. The Divine, whatever is your belief."

"So, if there's a creator at work who can create the miracles of nature and the superior mind-blowing vastness of the cosmos, do you think placing me back into my cold body, jump starting my heart and resetting my brain is beyond their capability? All I'm trying to say is would you ask a Formula One driver if he can drive a Ford Escort?"

"Oh, come off it. That's just too ridiculous a question to ponder!"

"Well then. You've just answered your own question."

"Oh. I see. Yes. Yes, I suppose in a way I have."

It is a concept that tests many a personal thought process and even has religions warring against each other.

No authority likes their belief system questioned and there have been those select individuals here on Earth that belonged to all manner of organisations only to come back to life after death to hand their membership cards in and walk away from all that they held dear.

Once they have *touched the face of God* as one surgeon put it, everything else falls into line and if you want to talk about a Spiritual Awakening then that's number one in the Spiritual charts. Nothing can surpass that.

I personally have never experienced an NDE however I have researched a multitude of accounts and books relating to the subject.

One of the best was Emanuel Swedenborg's Heaven & Hell. This is the bible of NDE accounts (in my opinion) and I say this not because it's the most important. It is simply written in such a fashion that it tests the hardiest of book junkies. It's a lot like the original Shakespeare. It does take some re-reading to get your head around.

However, there is help at hand! There is a non-profit organisation, The Swedenborg Foundation which promotes Spirituality and living a good and loving purposeful life. Well worth looking at is also a lovely guy named Curtis Childs who seats an online show where he has guests that discuss excerpts of the book Heaven & Hell. I would like to think that these are going to be available for years to come.

EMANUEL SWEDERBORG

He was a Swedish Scientist, philosopher, theologian and mystic best known for his book: Heaven and Hell (1758).

Swedenborg had a prolific career as an inventor and scientist. At age 53, he entered into a spiritual phase in which he began to experience dreams and visions, beginning on Easter weekend of 6th April 1744.

This culminated in a 'spiritual awakening', in which he received revelation that he was appointed by the Lord to write The *Heavenly Doctrine* to reform Christianity.

According to *The Heavenly Doctrine* the Lord had opened Swedenborg's spiritual eyes, so that from then on he could freely visit heaven and hell and talk with angels, demons and other spirits; and the Last Judgment had already occurred, in 1757.

For the remaining twenty eight years of his life, Swedenborg wrote eighteen published theological works, and several more which were unpublished. He termed himself a "Servant of the Lord Jesus Christ" in *True Christian Religion*, a work he published himself. Some followers of *The Heavenly Doctrine* believe that, of his theological works, only those which Swedenborg published himself are fully divinely inspired.

He was quite a man. I suppose there are those who will say that he could have made the whole thing up, however eighteen books and 28 years - that's some crazy hoax. Why would you do that? But on the other hand, Leonardo Da Vinci painted the famous Shroud of Christ. That was a true masterpiece of the almost impossible from a reverse negative aspect and, what was the point of that? Or, is it the real shroud? Did Jesus survive his crucifixion and actually walk out of the tomb as some have suggested? Escaped to France where he was hunted. Where DID his body actually go?

Leonardo Da Vinci always used to answer a question with a question. "Is it logical?" In the end, until you return home to your ultimate truth, you'll just have to go with what you think 'feels' right. But Leonardo has a very good viewpoint. If it isn't logical, that 'should' assist your judgement and elimination process.

I once read through a personal account of one of my friend's NDEs and was totally transfixed with what it explained. When she sent me her NDE account and I first read it, I will be completely honest I just had to sit in complete silence for a while. I felt as if I'd momentarily stopped on life's level crossing; glanced left only to be instantly smashed into by a Celestial High Speed Train and it threw me five hundred metres from whence I stood.

I don't like to express reaction to that account using normal phrases like 'jaw dropping' because all known phrases and adjectives have been used up here on Earth to describe events like the motorcycle stunt man jumping the Grand Canyon or, the magic trick where the lion completely vanishes upon being put in the cage when the cover is removed. This is all Earth stuff and the findings of Lorna and Swedenborg that we have just read was not of this time and place.

Not of Earth or our realm. It was Heavenly, God, Jesus and concepts whilst we are trapped inside our bodies, far too incredibly profound to even contemplate. To believe whole heartedly is wonderful but, when you listen to a human being talk of touching the very flesh of Jesus? It sends shivers of something so indescribable down the very core of my being.

That's the bit where I know what I'm reading is true. That's why I hold no judgement or make a conscious decision as to the authenticity of what it is I am reading. Because like I have said within this book a few times already, it is essentially the message about your Spiritual Sat Nav, go with the feeling.

How does it make you feel? Does it resonate with you?

- Do not believe with your eyes alone. They are projectors as well as viewers.

- Do not believe with your hearing alone or your touch.

- Do not believe what you experience with even a combination of all three. Simply check with your energy. Quite often though, your energy will check in with you way before you've taken a step back to ascertain just how you feel. It's one step ahead of you. Trust me! Do not follow roads already carved out by others. Go with your own feelings for they belong to you and you are actually God.

There are a whole multitude of beautifully written books covering NDE personal experiences out there. You won't have to look very far from where you found this book to see that they are in fact becoming more and more popular.

They need to be though. Humanity is (in my opinion) at a vast cliff edge right now, and those whom are being sent back have the kind of messages we so desperately need to hear if we are to believe in God's love for us, for ourselves.

If by chance, you're already a seasoned IANDS (International Association for Near Death Studies) member or you have already read up on another NDE account, I hope you have found some comfort in the reading that we are indeed 'eternal beings'. Our lives are magnificent journeys of creation and experiencing, learning and loving. We do not die. We live on. One day, we shall return home and when that day comes we will rejoice in our hearts for the return to the light of divine love - our true home.

CHAPTER FIFTEEN

Final Breath

"The biggest lie we are ever told, is that we die."

There will come a period in your life where ultimately it will be time to say goodbye *'for now'* to someone very dear to your heart. Someone you love. It doesn't have to be your mother or father... your brother or sister. It may even be your pet dog or cat. Dealing with 'death' *(as main stream society views it)* can be the ultimate test of your spiritual core being.

There will be that one statement that someone will quote and don't be surprised if it isn't spoken within your earshot as is sometimes the case.

"Why did God allow them to die? If there's a God why didn't he save them?"

Each person's natural response to death is a transition curve. It begins with shock, then devastating anger. Then complete sadness followed by different avenues of emotions according to how each of us views death. Although that transition curve can actually be swapped about. Everyone is different. For some, it can appear that they're completely fine with it and outwardly there's very little anger or sadness and very few tears.

I have found dealing with *the concept of* death a whole lot easier through learning about who I really am and trying to be more spiritual throughout my life.

I have confided in my mother that I really don't feel comfortable about attending her funeral when that day arrives and would only do it because 'not to' would start a war between me and my brothers.

This is what I told her:

"I know exactly where you're going Mum. I know you'll be free of all hurt and pain and you'll be having a ball; free and whole again, vibrant, meeting back up with your Sister and Mum. I will be so happy for you. But it's going to be tough because everyone else will be focused on that wooden box believing that you're actually in there dead and cold.

They'll all want to paint the world in black and it'll all be tears of sadness because that's the end. Death, darkness, sadness and then anger; I hate it - I loathe it.

I want to do the opposite Mum. I want to gather everyone together and say, "Hey, let's throw a massive party and wear bright vibrant colours! Black is totally out! Let's have loud music on and dance the night away to celebrate your promotion. You can be there too, joining in!"

However sometimes in life, you simply have to acknowledge and respect other's views and how they want to deal with losing loved ones; because to them that's what it means. Losing loved ones, never to be the same again. You will have to balance your own spirituality and belief system about celestial realms, don't be tempted to turn your core beliefs on as a defence weapon against the personal anger of those who are trying their best to accept and deal with what's happened.

There is no defence required. You do not have to argue that this death of the body is only a temporary physical absence. People's lives are literally turned upside-down when they lose their loved ones and it is the test of tests but there *is* something you can do. There is an answer to this. Be their rock, listen to their words. Be their comfort, even if you too are feeling sad, don't talk. Just listen.

During very stressful and challenging times of deep loss, this can be where your spiritual growth can be used to very good effect by being the rock for others and yes, by all means, *should* you be questioned quietly and calmly with a few tears; *"Do you think they're in heaven? Does heaven exist?"* This is your cue. Only then should you open the doorway to this highly sensitive subject at such a powerful time. It may come up and it is your choice as to how you approach it.

For every person wanting to approach this topic, there may well be another who feels that it's also the right time to chastise you for your belief in the afterlife.

They've just said goodbye to their loved ones and it's hurting like hell and they desperately need alcohol or a punch bag. It's their way of releasing their frustration because you appear to be handling this with a level of clarity and calm to which they cannot relate.

You're not in any way trying to prove anything but this isn't the case as they might see it. It's often a cruel and bizarre situation to be in. It can bring on resentment and it has the capacity to get extremely nasty depending on just how you react.

For me, this is the grand-daddy of all tests. You have to walk away from it. It is that simple. Do not engage in conflict. Do not rise to anger. You will fail miserably, that I can guarantee.

Whilst you're in your own comfort zone, you'll be fine. Once your family turn on you through sheer frustration or resentment, it is a very potent energy and *fight or flight* adrenaline will crush all spirituality and all manner of historic feuding will surface. It just won't end well, so walk away.

Someone once asked me what subject I was passionate about. You know, that *'ice breaker'* question from a total stranger sitting opposite you at your friend's wedding. The lottery of possibilities coming back at them, are quite exciting.

"Death," I said. Oh, wait!... and Legionnaires' disease. That's my career. Which oddly enough results in death? Huh! Never really thought about that until now!"

There was a sort of uncomfortable silence

"Okay then, moving swiftly on..."

It wasn't particularly received with the kind of enthusiasm which you would expect, however *it is* quite understandable really when you consider social views and teachings about this grim topic. Your final breath. The end. But here's the thing though, that's just it in a nutshell. Death. The end. Finished. Done.

Well, no. not really. Not at all.

The majority of people on this earth all view death as the big bad taboo that should never be uttered or discussed, and upon someone you know or love dying, you shall dress in depressing black *(other colours are available)* and be very sad and gloomy because they've gone.

I get the *gone* bit. I really do, please don't have me down as some sort of uncompassionate moron void of empathy and feeling, because believe me, I get sad just like anyone else, but having to say goodbye to my loved ones won't leave me asking questions or feeling confused. Death isn't going to change who I am. But to me death isn't the end. If anything, it's birth camouflaged as death.

Someone wrote. *"The greatest day of your life is when you're born. The saddest is when you die!"*

You think? I would argue this is back to front. I would say when you're born it's all total confusion. Reliance on Mum and non-stop questions Learning, guessing, trying to figure things out. Oh, I've wet myself again for the 400th time and what on earth is that stench? What are they saying, I can't communicate back?

That doesn't really stop until you're about 35 years of age. Death though? That's a party. Don't get me wrong I'm not promoting it and I sure don't want to die yet. I've got plenty sill left to do. Life is a gift. But I'm saying that once you're ready, and it's time or even if you are seen to be 'taken' suddenly, then the journey back home commences with a little cinematic stop on route and finally once the admin is all done you'll be back in the bliss of Source. So, what does actually happen when you die? *(I prefer the term 'pass' more).*

There have been many books and articles, endless studies and accounts through Near Death Experience (NDE's) and out of body experiences which basically all paint a pattern, and I will take you through some typical questions and answers.

DOES DEATH HURT?

That's a toughie but I can tell you from the accounts I've read and from my own experience of the psychology of pain that it would appear not to be so.

Firstly, I can tell you that I have had quite a number of what you would term *'household accidents'* during my life so far. You know the ones… Shut my finger in the door, paper cut at the tip of my finger and scalded my hand with boiling kettle water. *Ouch.*

The latter all had one undeniable characteristic about them on close observation. They hurt like hell and I turned the air blue, but I've also had other much more severe accidents. One in particular was life threatening when I was 14 years old.

I was hit by a car in Cheriton where I used to hang out as a teenager with friends. The car slammed into me tossing me over its roof and I landed five meters away with a broken leg. But here's the oddest thing about that, I recall the moments 'post-accident' with extreme clarity. It never hurt. Not a bit! I didn't feel anything at all and I do not actually remember the event until I came round to find myself lying on the pavement with people standing around me with two women attempting to come to my aid. I was later to find out that those two women were trained nurses at the Victoria Hospital in Folkestone and I wish I could thank them today for all that they did for me then.

There is a Spirit Science theory that suggests that when the human body is struck violently the Spirit of that person is removed from the physical body momentarily, to protect the soul. In an account of a NDE the driver of a vehicle explained that when his crash occurred he was suddenly able to watch it in a split second prior to the actual impact as if *'his Spirit had been wrenched from his body'* as he observed from above.

It wasn't until he had completed a journey of exploration and information back in the Spirit Realm and subsequently told *'It's not your time, you must return'* that he found himself lying under the truck he had hit, still beside what remained of his motorcycle with a paramedic shouting *'I think I can see his eyes and mouth moving, I think he's still with us!"*

He then explained that a pain came with the sensation of returning to his body and it wasn't good. Not at all. So, to sum up, I have decided personally that to a certain degree, we all worry about death because of the anticipation of the pain. Death is such a powerful word and I think we're all subconsciously paranoid that surely death will mean 'ultimate pain'.

It's almost an assumed gradient or measurement. If you prick your finger with a thorn, it's only a tiny pain and who hasn't had a cat claw get stuck in their finger? The pain is just horrendous!

So, what about death when you're ill with a terminal diagnosis of cancer and its long and drawn out? Death is seen as tragic enough whether sudden or otherwise. If you know of or love someone who fits this description because they are suffering in pain and you are aware that they are in the very final days of their lives I would like to say I'm sorry because I know all too well the feeling of helplessness is all too gripping. It's as if you join them in their suffering because there really isn't anything you can do or say that will make it better.

You have my love and compassion. My thoughts and blessings. So please be strong and know this: There is only love and joy in the Kingdom of God and this sadness and pain will surely pass. Then rejoice for they are finally free of the chains of the body and the pain. *They are home.*

The majority of NDEs will surely be accounts of a journey to Spirit and a return to the physical body by people of all backgrounds and ages. I would dare to suggest based on my research that they are usually very much like Lorna's story which I have mentioned. An everyday person with no particular issues or cares other than daily concerns and then boom! A car crash or lightning strike happens.

There have been a select few stories though by people who were diagnosed with terminally ill diseases like cancer, E. coli of the brain and a whole cavalcade of serious illnesses. The likes of which doctors will always state are terminal. That means without insulting anyone 'The end of the line!'

So just how did a select few come back from what surely is always considered the 'fait accompli'? If their bodies are riddled with malignant tumours and their brains infested with bacteria? Surely that's irreversible? It would appear not. An act of God? That's for you to decide. *Or feel is right,* but what about natural death through old age along with other well-known issues.

I'm going to stereotype now. A man of 97 years who has lost all cognitive ability and is in a more or less very poor 'vegetative state'. Not physically able to move through years of degenerative disorder and quite literally and sadly, waiting to pass. This scenario is long and drawn out. It sees the person in a state of being able to actually be part of that death process and here's what I have learnt over the years about the sequence of events.

Nobody actually dies alone, there will arrive a window where you will receive visits. Now I'm not talking about the ones from family and friends who've moved hell and high water around their work schedule to keep bringing you grapes and flowers. These visits will be from those who you know and love that have passed into Spirit before you. To put it bluntly, old friends departed will quite literally be coming out of the walls.

Here's a question for you, did you ever visit someone who was in a situation where, without doubt, you knew they were waiting to pass? Did you visit them and hear any of the following examples?

"Well, Grandad thought he could see Aunt Susan and was talking to her. Silly old beggar! The medication has obviously had an effect on him. He's seeing ghosts now. I saw him today and do you know he actually looked quite well? As if he's getting better?"

When it's *'time'* you will begin to experience extreme paranormal events like visitations from people who you know couldn't possibly be in this world because you personally went to their funeral some forty years ago, and their body was cremated. Your visitors will know and will have been waiting years, to come and see you. They will ask you if you're ready to leave. Have you ever heard the following statement?

"Well Dad had been terminally ill for some time. We got the call from his nurses to say that we should all get to the hospital because it wouldn't be long. We did so and all held his hand and cried and told him how much we loved him. We all went for a coffee to give him some rest and the nurse came to the coffee machine to tell us the sad news that whilst we were out of the room, he let go. He died."

He did indeed let go, once he had been allowed time to say his farewells to his loved ones. Let go and took the hand of his visitors who had come to walk and guide him home. Quite beautiful when you think about it.

So, what now? You pass. You give your body back. Where do you go and what happens? And will my step-dad who was horrible to me be there? I don't want that.

Right then. A subject that has indeed been well covered and written about but has with it a caveat.

Everyone's journey into the 'afterlife' is different for their own personal reasons. You recall I said, "What you think ~ you create."

Well that applies more so to Spirit than ever. It's an element of Spirit Science that we have been gifted with as humans to use as our life tool in a much lower vibration. We mirror our spiritual family back home however we operate at a much slower speed. When Spirits think – it is done. When we think, it takes some time to manifest.

You will find that what has manifested on our Earth has also manifested in Spirit. Many of the great inventions by talented gifted scientists are not just random thoughts by an individual human being with nothing better to do. Those who focus on invention here will draw in a collaboration of Spirit team inventors without them consciously being aware and occasionally thoughts inside the minds of the human inventors are injected with Spirit thought.

Elvis has left the building!

So, one minute, you're bracing yourself for the end and just when you've considered the very thought of it, you've passed and now find yourself hovering around looking down on what you identify as 'you'. But it's presenting a rather peculiar quandary. How can that really be? If you still feel like you?

Remember that if you are now looking at you, every inch; every atom of your core being you will have to summon up all the rational thinking that you have ever known in a bid to accept that:

'You're not dead but, that is still the 'you' that was alive as a human hologram below.

You now feel a million times healthier and vibrant than in your teens and on your best EVER day. Being back in that body would feel restrictive. Like trying to swim through treacle. It's at this juncture that based on the multitude of accounts from NDE experiences, the different scenarios between leaving and departing the earthly ether and transitioning into the final Spiritual World has an abundance of variety.

For some, it has meant a transfer into complete darkness first. Generally, I have found through my research that this tends to occur if you have spent a life denying the existence of a loving God, which implies a denial of love. This will always end well so long as the experiencer calls out to be 'saved' from this darkness. I can tell you that in all accounts, this has been the case. What happens then is an angel will appear and take their hand only to guide them through a tunnel and eventually toward a small speck of brilliant light which grows as it becomes closer.

This light is brighter than our sun, however does not present discomfort to those who seek and want to embrace it. It isn't hanging in the time space like our sun does, it is just there. No night or day. No cycles. No time. Just light and love. Some humans who pass go straight to the tunnel experience. The whole nine yards. They travel through it, often finding accompaniment of either loved ones or angelic beings. This will end with arrival within that same 'place of light'.

Then, depending on each individual's circumstance, they may go to a resting place like heaven's version of a hospital ward if they as humans died from a long illness. It will be important that they then come around and gain strength within their real home and are counselled by angels and soul family. If they died as the result of a sudden impact and do not actually realise the enormity of the situation, many angels will come to them and counsel them in a bid to get them to understand what has happened and that they have passed across.

This can be quite traumatic for an individual soul who has great difficulty realising what has happened. It is why I stated earlier about the importance of understanding our Life Science and then, Spirit Science. If you are ready and cognitively prepared for the other side, despite accounts like this being probably a little off grid, you'll get the general idea. I'm pretty sure I've explained a kind of "Death for Dummies" handbook version here.

THE LIFE REVIEW

Given that everyone has arrived whether they were ill on Earth for years or they were struck by a lightning bolt, all will then go through what is termed the 'Life Review'.

Now I have stated that I have never had an NDE, despite not knowing where I went in the short time I was struck by a car, but something totally bizarre happened to me shortly prior to that incident and it has kind of bothered me ever since.

I was at RAF Manston with 617 Squadron ATC gliding club. I'd been going for some time and today was going to be the day I flew solo. I was a very eager teenager. It was a massive deal for me. Remember, I hadn't yet taken any serious exams. Too young for secondary school O Levels. Too young for a car or motorcycle licence. But here I was, just a kid, about to take control of an aircraft. So, it began well. Take off turned into 'pole bending' and I had to ease off as I levelled out on the steel cable which was about 950' below.

I levelled out and carried out my cable detach with a double tug on the lever and a dip of the nose. All was well. I made a 270° turn and then drifted toward the point where I'd nose down to pick up speed for the final turn in. I remember it all going super smooth, it felt brilliant to be the master of my own piece of sky. This flight is a mere five minutes but what a rush. That's where I kind of checked out and have no real idea of how I came to land in the manner in which I did. But that isn't really the weird bit.

As I came in on finals I do remember I selected spoilers to lose massive amounts of height as I reached the fence. I think if I had to guess, I'd say I left the spoilers on as I turned in and winged over sharply to come into land. I just remember with utter horror the aircraft yawing massively nose left 30° off centre line and feeling like I was going to see the tail plane any second. It became disorientating and confusing. Suddenly I had forgotten how to fly; it was as if a hypnotist had clicked his fingers.

The sun was beginning to set, shining straight into my eyes. It was close to 6pm when I experienced a very odd almost paranormal sensation. Despite 'knowing' that my aircraft and I were in trouble I almost didn't care and felt as if nothing actually mattered. I then saw my entire life up until that point quite literally flash before me. Just as the expression states, it literally 'flashed before my eyes,' and left me stunned. But as quickly as it all started to fold on the approach to land, it then unfolded and to my complete shock and surprise I found myself flying at very high speed, very straight and 6' above the landing strip to make a perfect text-book landing down by the hangars.

When I met up with my Instructor he just looked at me and said, *"Well, that went alright from down here Noel. I have to say though, you'd make a great aerobatics pilot with those snappy moves. Quite brilliant young man. Well done."*

My Mum collected me in the car and we drove home to Hythe in relative silence. Stupidly, I never went back and two years later I joined the RAF. To this day as I write this book, and after talking with my friend, I'm pondering a question. Do I go and see someone? Do I lie on that bed and be regressed to that moment? And what about that car accident I had where I can't remember anything?

A life review is exactly what it says on the tin. Your life, reviewed. As Billy Cohen (Billy Fingers) told his sister Annie in the book *"The Afterlife of Billy Fingers"*, "You get to review your life when you pass, so make sure it's interesting!"

There is though, a catch. Yeah. Kind of a big one and some of us, well, I should think *all* of us aren't going to particularly like. This is the section where in religious circles preachers will tell you that you will be judged, cast into brimstone and hellfire for eternity and made to suffer indescribable pain because an all loving God has a dark side and can be fickle like that.

Hellfire and damnation, in a word or two. Utter Tosh!

What 'actually' takes place you will be relieved to know is that yes, you get to see the whole thing. A movie from the seconds you were born to the second you were escorted away from Earth back to the celestial theatre in which you now stand.

But here's the thing. You get to FEEL the cause and effect. You get to FEEL the emotions of those who you have wronged. I say wronged, but in truth, it's anything you have said or done to cause upset to others. There isn't really wrong and right, more like cause and effect. This can be a single word like 'No,' when it matters the most to someone or, when you lost your temper and lashed out verbally and physically assaulting another when they were being kind. But hey, that's life.

On Earth, to fail is to be human. It is exactly why you chose to come here. The real cherry on the top of this cake is that you actually experience all of the emotions of those who you have interacted with, positive or negative. You get to FEEL the emotions of those who you interact with and then, at the same time, others who were at the receiving end of the ripple effect.

So, who judges you? YOU DO!

I was once asked by a sergeant in the RAF to write my own assessment. My first reaction was one of relief. But that soon turned to horror. Try and write your own assessment. Try and look yourself in the eye in a mirror and tell yourself you're a great person and you're as good as you think you are. It's actually really hard and quite an uncomfortable experience. I ended up turning my boss down and told him to do it. I found out the hard way that when we're brutally honest with ourselves, it can be scathing.

During your life review expect tears, plenty of them. Complete empathy for those to whom you caused pain and suffering, because you get to see their souls. If you had that ability back in body, you'd never in a million years have acted the way you did. When you see their soul, you also see a reflection of yours. You see God. God is Love of the purest love of all.

However, there are also tears of joy and total elation. You get to see how wonderful your actions were and how they rippled across the Universe and affected others. So, it isn't all that bad. This is the point where I'd have to start to invent and make it all up because choices are then made by the Spirit for the Spirit. Nobody sends you anywhere. You send yourself.

It's my understanding that where this Life Review takes place is like Heaven Reception. You reside there for as long as you wish for reasons only known to you. Some in books have coined the phrase 'Summer Realm' to describe it. It is actually almost like a mirror of the earth you just departed. The difference being it is more beautiful and it has no hatred or war. Hunger or homeless. Many have said: "As above, so below."

There are according to books which I have researched, several realms of residence and the closest one to our dimension is that which is termed the 'lower realm.' It has also been called the 'Dark Realm'. Religion and church followers will know it as 'hell.'

If you are a soul who lives for love and the compassion for others at any cost to yourself, you are going to be escorted through or, around the lower realms as they can be extremely frightening and intimidating. Many NDE experiences have referred to accounts stating that the tunnel you travel through is almost through the centre of this lower realm and if you were to look deeply into each side as you pass you can see lost souls and other alien entities. It is the reason why it is so dark. No light can exist there and that's just how the souls who reside there want it.

They're not in any pain. Far from it. They feel like you would on holiday. They rejected the light at heaven's door and after being offered the light of the Holy Spirit they *(given that you have free will)* chose the darkness. Having free will doesn't stop when you pass across. If you want to be how society would describe 'evil' then that is your choice. God will want you to accept his love but if you cannot, then you are free to travel to a realm of like-minded souls.

So, in this next paragraph, you simply have to reverse the logic. Upon accepting the love and light of the Holy Spirit you then go somewhere quite special. Souls who are like-minded in thought, vibration, ambition, will group together in their own heaven. Just as those who enjoy pulling the legs off spiders do theirs. Everyone who dies doesn't ultimately end up in the same place. Again, I wish to stress that everything I have stated here is based on others accounts and my research.

Remember that saying *"Your vibe attracts your tribe?"*

Well so it continues in the celestial heavens.

Uncle Frank who used to beat you won't necessarily be there to greet you. It has quite often been stated by Spiritual Mediums for example that Uncle Jack and Bill who detested each other here on earth have both changed. They have met in Spirit and have sorted it all out. They are actually now very good friends. (Much to the gasps of family members).

So now you go off more than likely to a massive reunion party by your soul family who rejoice at your return and celebrate your life with you.

Some have said they were allowed to experience this in part, as an example, or a message to bring back to Earth validating our Eternity. They explained there were literally hundreds of beautiful souls wearing their 'bodies of light' and dressed according to their time period of which they last lived a physical life.

The experiencer would describe that they knew them but initially didn't know how, as it was still too early, and elements of the physical body were still not yet fully gone. I don't know about you, but I find the whole thing about the Spirit World fascinating.

The concept of Halls of Learning can be compared to the Victoria & Albert Museum in London. In Spirit it's a place very similar with vast endless historical artefacts which not only cover Earth but everywhere else and who knows how many other planets and in what form we incarnate? There are also the Akashic Records, another subject that has been well documented.

THE AKASHIC RECORDS

Edgar Cayce on the Akashic Records

"The Akashic Records or "The Book of Life" can be equated to the Universe's super computer system. It is this system that acts as the central storehouse of all information for every individual who has ever lived upon the Earth. More than just a reservoir of events, the Akashic Records contain every deed, word, feeling, thought, and intent that has ever occurred at any time in the history of the world. Much more than simply a memory storehouse.

However, these Akashic Records are interactive in that they have a tremendous influence upon our everyday lives, our relationships, our feelings and belief systems, and the potential realities we draw toward us. Upon time and space is written the thoughts, the deeds, the activities of an entity – as in relationships to its environs, its hereditary influence; as directed – or judgement drawn by or according to what the entity's ideal is. Hence, as it has been oft called, the record is God's Book of Remembrance; and each entity, each soul – as the activities of a single day of an entity in the material world – either makes same good or bad or indifferent, depending upon the entity's application of self towards that which is the ideal manner for the use of time, opportunity and the expression of that for which each soul enters a material manifestation.

The interpretation then as drawn here is with the desire and hope that, in opening this for the entity, the experience may be one of helpfulness and hopefulness."

(Edgar Cayce Reading 1650-1)

It's no exaggeration to state that the computer has transformed (and is still in the process of transforming) the entire planet.

Whether that's technology, transportation, communication, education, or entertainment, the computer age has revolutionized the globe and the ways in which we understand and interact with one another. No segment of modern society has gone unaffected. The amount of information now stored in computer memory and crossing the Internet highway daily is literally unfathomable.

And yet, this vast complex of computer systems and collective databases cannot begin to come close to the power, the memory, or the omniscient recording capacity of the Akashic Records.

BIBLICAL REFERENCES: BOOK OF LIFE

Information about the Akashic Records ~ the Book of Life can be found in folklore, in myth, and throughout the Old and New Testaments. It is traceable at least as far back as the Semitic peoples and includes the Arabs, the Assyrians, the Phoenicians, the Babylonians, and the Hebrews.

Among each of these people was the belief that there was in existence some kind of celestial tablets which contained the history of humankind as well as all manner of spiritual information.

The first reference in Scripture to some unearthly volume is found in Exodus 32:32. After the Israelites had committed a most grievous sin by worshiping the golden calf, it was Moses who pleaded on their behalf, even offering to take full responsibility and have his own name stricken "out of thy book which thou hast written" in recompense for their deed.

Later, in the Old Testament, we learn that there is nothing about an individual that is not known in this same book. In Psalm 139, David refers to the fact God has written down everything about him and all the details of his life ~ even that which is imperfect and those deeds which have yet to be performed.

Akashic Records or "The Book of Life" for many is simply an imagery symbol of those destined for heaven and has its roots in the custom of recording genealogical records of names or perhaps early census taking. Traditional religion suggests that this book ~ either in literal or symbolic form ~ contains the names of all those who are worthy of salvation.

The Book is to be opened in connection with Divine Judgment (Dan. 7:10, Rev. 20:12). In the New Testament, those redeemed by Christ are contained within the Book (Philippians 4), those not found in the Book of Life will not enter the Kingdom of Heaven. As an interesting corollary, in the ancient world, a person's name was symbolic of his or her existence.

According to Sir James George Frazer, author of *The Golden Bough* – one of the most extensive volumes on world mythology – there was such a bond between one's name and one's existence "that magic may be wrought on a man just as easily as through his name as through his hair, his nails, or any other material part of his person."

In ancient Egypt, to blot a name out of a record was equivalent to destroying the fact that the person had ever existed. It really shouldn't be a surprise to learn that Spirit has its own version of the World Wide Web. Everything documented. Everything in human, or other terms that was, is and shall be. Otherwise, what on Earth *(or other planets)* is the point?

That is it though, as far as death goes, it's a pretty awesome experience to be marvelled at and the possibilities are limitless once you go 'home' to whence you came. Life on earth to quote our friend Billy is simply a stopover.

But then, I guess after a brief rest and gossip back there in Spirit, you'll make flight arrangements and plans with other souls and before you know it... Get yourself talked into some other project by your family and off you go all over again. And why not!

I am love, and my mission is to live and experience a life in accordance with love.

CONCLUSION

Earth (Gaia) is important amongst all of our possible places of physical learning and experiencing. Mother Earth, if destroyed, would send a shock wave of 'implication' like a Universal Tsunami ripple effect throughout the entire massive expanse and realms of finite reality.

Basically, speaking in terms that we would relate to, the whole of our existence in Spirit would then have to undergo great change. It has never been more critical to share the love, to increase this loving and compassionate vibration here on this beautiful miracle called Earth. Our home. While we're here, the only one we have and if you were to ask me if I actually believe all that stuff about alien races and ETs visiting our Earth? I can tell you this much:

I am a child of God and I carry within my heart the seed of the Divine Creator. I am love, and my mission is to live and experience a life in accordance with love. Nothing more. Upon my physical death in years to come, if asked if I could take a slight detour on my journey to heaven and go to a planet similar to the one humans call Earth, one that's in deep trouble and requires help. That I travel there to be born and grow up to help increase the vibration to a point where hatred and war, fear and oppression become the minority, and peace and harmony has the opportunity to live and thrive - I'd do it without question.

Maybe, just maybe I've already agreed to do it here by writing my thoughts, feelings and experiences here. Now there's a thought! Now then, go and get that life you signed up for!

All the very best to you and all that you hold dear, may God shine his Divine Blessing of love and light on you.

All my love and appreciation for being here with me,

Noel

FOLLOWING THE B ROAD

Begin Your Daily Journey of Discovery

1. Begin to explore meditation. Find one that you feel comfortable with. Make time for it, whether this is at 5am or in the middle of a busy day. Try it. Don't worry about being 'aware' of doing it. Just be. You will, in time begin to find yourself. It'll all become perfectly natural after a while. The benefits will soon become quite clear!

2. Take time to sit and think about your social media profile. *(If you have one?)* Just take a look at who's on it. Ask those uncomfortable questions. Do they add, or remove value towards your life? If they're always moaning and being the 'New Age Empath' or the victim, it might be time to let them go. Chances are they'll not even notice that you've got rid of them from your profile as they'll be so wrapped up in their day-to-day stuff.

3. Have a look at your health. Take yourself off to the doctor and ask for an MOT. Why not? You want to know if there's anything going on below the surface that may have a direct effect on your emotions and your day-to-day thinking. High blood pressure, sugar levels, water retention etc. But be careful when it's time to dish out

those coloured pills. They don't fix all problems. A change of lifestyle can quite often sort out mundane common health issues.

4. Take a look at what you've unconsciously slipped into watching on your television. Or, more importantly, watch it as you normally would and mark down on a piece of paper a line every time someone is negative, then decide what you're going to do about it. You may think you're enjoying the programs when in fact you're not enjoying it. You're addicted to the negativity.

5. Ask yourself if you're being honest with your friends. Are they real friends? Ask yourself who you're swimming the Channel for on a regular basis, but who wouldn't cross a puddle for you? This doesn't mean you should stop being who you are. It means waking up to the real facts of where and why those who you associate with as friends are around you.

6. Your empathy and compassion for others is to be applauded, but be mindful of being used up and worn out. One thing is to be the 'best friend'. It's another to not realise who's using you for their own selfish benefit and who's not.

7. Look inside you to find out what you enjoy. What makes you happy? Pursue it with a warrior like spirit and go do it!

8. Find somewhere that means something to you spiritually. A water fountain in the park. It could be a mountain trek,

canal walk or a waterfall. It can even be a room in your house that has Frankincense and Myrrh burning and ambient mood lighting. Anywhere that allows you to recharge. A retreat for you to find yourself and shake of excess stale energy. A place to have a mini-meditation perhaps.

9. I like to go out on my mountain bike. That for me is where I kind of meditate. Just me and my bike. Don't forget, you can take your partner with you. Some of the best and creative conversations begin in places of spiritual beauty and stillness.

10. Have a think about what you'd like to do to help your fellow human beings - a token gesture of kindness.

It could be doing the shopping for an elder who is struggling or walking their dog. It might be an annual visit to your local soup kitchen for the homeless. Why not start up a back-pack homeless campaign? They're a superb idea. Get people in your area via a social media campaign or your local church to fill an old or second-hand ruck sack or back pack, with simple spare items like socks, jumpers, coats, hats, compact sleeping bags and tins of soup and a torch. The list can be anything that you can fit into a pack.

11. Food. Begin to look at what you're eating and if there's excess? Ask for what reason? You'll normally find it's a substitution for something.

12. Lethal man-made chemicals are now so common it's frightening. Begin by eliminating GMO (genetically modified organism) foods. Try to eat green foods and naturally grown produce. Not always easy and can become expensive but try where you can. Generally have a well-balanced, healthy diet.

13. If you smoke? At least think about the effects on other people especially if you have children or grandchildren. If you can't do it for you, can you do it for them? I smoked for over thirty years and I eventually gave up.

14. Chemicals. Fluoride. Don't drink tap water unless it's filtered. Purchase fluoride free toothpaste. Steer well clear of sweeteners like aspartame.

15. Have you got outstanding issues with people who you've decided are best left alone, because then it might just *fade away and be forgotten?* Go and find them. Do that. Find them and forgive them. Whether it is by post, email, text or face to face. It will be the most liberating thing you will ever do, and you'll actually feel your soul and spirit applaud you. It will feel like you've been plugged into the national grid. Believe me.

16. Finally, remember one thing. You're doing your best, okay? You're doing your best within the resource and amongst the personal circumstances that you find yourself currently in. Just remember that today maybe utterly crap. Tomorrow really is the start of a brand-new day. Tensions and frustrations are temporary. Problems remember, are

only your perception of the issue at hand. So, try and step back and take a breather. You'll be fine.

It's all going to be okay in the end.

If it isn't okay?

Then. It's not the end.

DAILY REMINDERS

A New Way of Thinking

- You will lose no light from your flame by lighting another's.
- Faith is invisible... But like Wi-Fi it has the power to connect you to that which you need.
- We perceive things... not as they are, but as we are. Your vibe will attract your tribe.
- Realigning your path to a spiritual one doesn't prevent you from seeing the darkness ...It merely assists you in knowing how to use it as a tool to grow.
- If God is all you have... you have all you really need.
- Just by being the real authentic you, means putting something extremely unique and special out into the world we live in.
- The only disability in life, is a negative attitude.
- Life is no accident ... your life is very much on purpose.
- What you think ...you become.
- Thoughts are energy... Everything that you think is a conversation with the Universe.
- You chose to be born here on Earth. It's your script. You run the show.
- Other peoples' opinions of you are actually none of your business.
- We only see what our eyes want us to believe.

- Be mindful about what you wish to buy and what you're being sold. Your personality and thinking soaks up traits from those who you hang out with. In a way, your persona attracts select elements of theirs.
- Be mindful of who you choose to associate with on a regular basis.
- Making a judgement about others isn't the issue. The issue is about treating others based on your initial judgement of them. How you treat others defines who you are, not who they are.
- Spiritual ego is the goal... Human ego is not.
- There is no such thing as a 'coincidence' in your life.
- You are meant to go through the bad stuff. Life isn't punishing you.
- You control your life. It doesn't happen to you. It happens for you.
- Never be so afraid of death that you can't live.
- Death isn't the end. Far from it. In many ways, you'll look back at it from the other side and view it as a beginning.
- Trust the Universe. It has your back and will always deliver if you believe that the dots will join up ahead of you.
- The Universal Law of Attraction isn't a cliché, it's real and what's more it is probably the most powerful force in the known Universe along with Love.
- Nobody ever got poor by giving. What you reap, you sow.
- Don't think that giving will create more wealth – that's not how it works!
- Choose to live in accordance with love and not fear.
- Be the change that you would like to see in others.
- Be mindful of associations or religions that promote division and separation.

- Separation is an illusion. We are all connected despite race, wealth, colour, religion.

- Don't be too hard on yourself. Life can be tough. You're doing the best you can.

- Try to forgive your enemies wherever you can.

- Try to meditate at least 20 minutes a day. If you haven't got the time because you're too busy, then you should take an hour when you can.

- You are God to your body's cells. You, have the power to heal yourself.

- There is no such thing as Hell. Only in your mind.

- Heaven (Home of Spirit) is very real. It's your true home. If you're unwilling to face questioning your beliefs, then you will never know if you are following a truth or a lie.

- Steer clear of newspapers, TV news, and negative news on social media.

- Always look for the positive spark within the framework of a negative situation.

- If you're currently going through hell?... Keep going.

- The more wisdom you attain and more conscious knowledge, the crazier you will appear to others.

- If you live for your own happiness, you will be chasing your tail. If you live to make others happy, only then will you truly find happiness within yourself.

- Life is a divine gift and the moment you decide to treat it as such... It will become one.

NOEL RECOMMENDS

Must see YouTube videos:

- Everything by Alan Watts
- David Icke – YouTube seminar presentations
- Abraham (Esther) Hicks – Any of her clips on YouTube
- Eckhart Tolle – Any of his books, clips.
- Russell Brand (Spiritual) Mostly seen on 'The Trews.'
- Jim Carrey (Spiritual) mostly advertised on social media. Especially the Class of 2014 speech.
- Swedenborg Foundation OTLE. Search on YouTube.
- The Journey of Purpose TJOP. You Tube.
- Carl Sagan – 'The Pale Blue Dot.' Clip on YouTube.

Great Books:

- The Afterlife of Billy Fingers by Annie Kagan
- And the Truth Shall Set You Free. (All books by David Icke)
- Life in the World Unseen by Anthony Borgia
- Heaven & Hell – Emanuel Swedenborg
- Glimpses of Eternity by Dr Raymond Moody

Must Watch Films:

- The Shawshank Redemption
- The Fisher King
- Good Will Hunting
- What Dreams May Come
- Sliding Doors
- Heaven & Earth
- Hero
- Hearts in Atlantis

ONE LAST NOTE

Its life Jim but not as we know it

The day the real Jim Carrey (actor of Dumb & Dumber, Pet Detective, and Liar-Liar) took a step forward, for me was a moment that melted my soul like no other.

I have admired his wit and his comedy since his very first appearance on screen. I feel like I always knew him. His ability to clown around and make fun of the absolute seriousness of life is a gift in itself and to us all. But one day he gave a speech and the cameras were rolling. This time though, we were all going to be in for a bit of a surprise. I ask you to watch the video if you can to receive the full impact and emotion of what it was Jim was saying that day to the class of 2014.

It wasn't just a statement of truth to one class, it was a beautiful, fantastic inspiring, and educational jaw dropping speech which I feel should always be remembered and associated with who Jim Carrey really is. *The real Jim Carrey – You Tube.*

Music - The Police: Spirits in the Material World

'Spirits in the Material World' has etched its authenticity and meaning into the fabric of my being for many years. It is a basic, clever but remarkable piece of art in my view which has an extremely deep subliminal message that we need to fix this broken system if we are to live the lives we truly want. It's also a fantastic song, in my humble opinion.

Spirits in the Material World

The Police

There is no political solution
To our troubled evolution
Have no faith in constitution
There is no bloody revolution

We are spirits in the material world
Are spirits in the material world
Are spirits in the material world
Are spirits in the material world

Our so-called leaders speak
With words they try to jail you
They subjugate the meek
But it's the rhetoric of failure

We are spirits in the material world
Are spirits in the material world
Are spirits in the material world
Are spirits in the material world

Where does the answer lie?
Living from day to day
If it's something we can't buy
There must be another way

We are spirits in the material world
Are spirits in the material world
Are spirits in the material world
Are spirits in the material world
Are spirits in the material world
Are spirits in the material world

This song is based on the writings of Hungarian author and philosopher Arthur Koestler after one of his books. Koestler believed that outside influences could destroy our spirit and restrict our thinking. The "spirits" and "ghosts" Koestler wrote about were the innate higher functions that often get lost in the "machine" created by governments and corporations. Sting explained the song's meaning in Lyrics by Sting:

"I thought that while political progress is clearly important in resolving conflict around the world, there are spiritual (as opposed to religious) aspects of our recovery that also need to be addressed. I suppose by 'spiritual' I mean the ability to see the bigger picture, to be able to step outside the narrow box of our conditional thinking."

Noel Hogan is a Visionary, Company Director, Teacher, Trainer, Spiritual Thinker, Writer and Counsellor. His mission is to inspire and motivate. Having travelled extensively he now lives in North Lincolnshire, England with his wife.

Trust Your Spiritual Sat Nav

E-Book Available

www.spiritualsatnav.com